Student Support Materials for AQA

AS Chemistry

Unit 2: Chemistry in Action

Authors: John Bentha   raham Curtis,

Geoffrey Ha   David Nicholls.

William Collins's dream of knowledge for all began with the publication of his first book in 1819. A self-educated mill worker, he not only enriched millions of lives, but also founded a flourishing publishing house. Today, staying true to this spirit, Collins books are packed with inspiration, innovation and practical expertise. They place you at the centre of a world of possibility and give you exactly what you need to explore it.

Collins. Freedom to teach.

Published by Collins
An imprint of HarperCollinsPublishers
77-85 Fulham Palace Road
Hammersmith
London
W6 8JB

Browse the complete Collins catalogue at
www.collinseducation.com

ISBN-13   978-0-00-726826-9

John Bentham, Colin Chambers, Graham Curtis, Geoffrey Hallas, Andrew Maczek and David Nicholls assert their moral right to be identified as the authors of this work.

British Library Cataloguing in Publication Data. A Catalogue record for this publication is available from the British Library.

Commissioned by Penny Fowler
Edited by Jane Glendening
Proof read by Patrick Roberts
Design by Newgen Imaging
Cover design by Angela English
Production by Arjen Jansen
Printed and bound in Hong Kong by Printing Express

Contents

3.2.1 Energetics

Enthalpy change ΔH

The **enthalpy change** of a system is the heat energy change at constant pressure. It is indicated by the symbol ΔH where Δ is the 'change in' or 'difference in' and H is the enthalpy.

When a system gives out heat energy to the surroundings, enthalpy is lost by the system so that ΔH is negative (**exothermic**).

When a system takes in heat from the surroundings, enthalpy is gained by the system so that ΔH is positive (**endothermic**).

Standard enthalpy changes occur at the standard pressure of 100 kPa (1 bar) and a stated temperature, usually taken as 298 K. The symbol $\Delta H^{\ominus}$ is used for standard enthalpy changes.

Elements and compounds are said to be in their **standard state** if they are in their normal, stable state at 298 K and 100 kPa. Where a compound such as water could be either a gas or a liquid under standard conditions, the physical state of the substance should be clarified by symbol or by explanation. For example $H_2O(l)$ refers to water in the liquid state, $H_2O(g)$ refers to water vapour (steam). Where elements exist in allotropic forms, the particular **allotrope** should be specified, for example C (graphite) or C(diamond). If the allotrope is not specified it is assumed to be the more stable form (graphite in the case of carbon).

Standard enthalpy of combustion $\Delta H_c^{\ominus}$

> **Definition**
>
> The **standard enthalpy of combustion** is defined as the enthalpy change, under standard conditions, when 1 mol of a substance is burned completely in oxygen, with all reactants and products in their standard states.

Standard conditions are usually taken as 100 kPa and 298 K; at this temperature, water is usually taken to be a liquid.

The enthalpy change is linked to an equation with state symbols. For example:

$$CH_4(g) + 2O_2(g) \rightarrow CO_2(g) + 2H_2O(l) \qquad \Delta H_c^{\ominus} = -890 \text{ kJ mol}^{-1}$$

Enthalpies of combustion are determined experimentally using a **calorimeter.**

Standard enthalpy of formation $\Delta H_f^{\ominus}$

> **Definition**
>
> The **standard enthalpy of formation** is defined as the enthalpy change, under standard conditions, when 1 mol of a compound is formed from its elements with all reactants and products in their standard states.

By definition, for an element the standard enthalpy of formation must be zero.

Examiners' Notes

The sign of the enthalpy change is taken from the point of view of the reaction. If the reaction gives out (loses) heat energy, the enthalpy change is negative. If the reaction takes in (gains) heat energy, the enthalpy change is positive.

Essential Notes

The symbol $\ominus$ shows that the change is measured under standard conditions.

Essential Notes

Accurate enthalpies of combustion are determined by an experiment in a bomb calorimeter. In a school laboratory it is possible to measure enthalpies of combustion using simple apparatus such as a 'spirit burner' but this usually gives values which are not sufficiently exothermic. The main error is due to an inability to measure the heat energy which is lost to the surroundings.

Examiners' Notes

For an element $\Delta H_f^{\ominus} = 0$.

The following is an example of a reaction for which the enthalpy change is the enthalpy of formation:

$$2Na(s) + C(graphite) + \frac{3}{2}O_2(g) \rightarrow Na_2CO_3(s) \quad \Delta H_f^{\ominus} = -1131 \text{ kJ mol}^{-1}$$

Enthalpies of formation are usually determined indirectly using Hess's law, as explained on pages 6–8, and can be found in data-book tables.

Calorimetry

The heat energy, q, required to change the temperature of a substance by an amount ΔT can be calculated using the expression:

$$q = m \times c \times \Delta T$$

where m is the mass of the substance and c is the specific heat capacity. Commonly, c is given with the units $\text{kJ K}^{-1} \text{kg}^{-1}$ which requires that m be expressed in kilograms and ΔT in kelvin, giving q the units kJ. For many chemical reactions in aqueous solution it can be assumed that the only substance heated is water, which has a specific heat capacity of $4.18 \text{ kJ K}^{-1} \text{kg}^{-1}$.

The heat energy, q, can be used to calculate an enthalpy change as shown in the two examples which follow.

Example

In an experiment, 1.00 g of methanol (CH_3OH) was burned in air and the flame was used to heat 100 g of water, which rose in temperature by 42.0 °C.

$$CH_3OH(l) + \frac{3}{2}O_2(g) \rightarrow CO_2(g) + 2H_2O(g)$$

Calculate the enthalpy change.

Answer

- Heat energy gained by the water

$$q = m \times c \times \Delta T$$
$$= 0.100 \times 4.18 \times 42.0$$
$$= 17.6 \text{ kJ}$$

- Heat energy lost by methanol

$$= -17.6 \text{ kJ}$$

- Moles of methanol burned

$$= \frac{\text{mass}}{M_r}$$
$$= \frac{1.00}{32.0} = 0.0313 \text{ mol}$$

- Enthalpy change per mole

$$\Delta H = \frac{\text{heat energy lost by methanol}}{\text{moles of methanol}}$$
$$= \frac{-17.6}{0.0313} \text{ kJ mol}^{-1}$$
$$= -563 \text{ kJ mol}^{-1}$$

Essential Notes

For the purpose of this calculation, heat losses are ignored and the heat absorbed by the water container is regarded as negligible.

Examiners' Notes

Note that the mass of water must be converted into kg (100 g = 0.100 kg) but that a temperature difference in degrees Celsius is the same as that in kelvins.

Examiners' Notes

Note the *negative* sign because the reaction is exothermic.

Example

In an insulated container, 50 cm^3 of 2.00 mol dm^{-3} HCl at 293 K were added to 50.0 cm^3 of 2.00 mol dm^{-3} NaOH also at 293 K. After reaction, the temperature of the mixture rose to 307 K.

$$HCl(aq) + NaOH(aq) \rightarrow NaCl(aq) + H_2O(l)$$

Calculate the enthalpy change.

Answer

- Temperature rise $\quad\quad\quad\quad \Delta T = 14.0$ K

- Heat energy gained
  by the water $\quad\quad\quad\quad q = m \times c \times \Delta T$

  $\quad\quad\quad\quad\quad\quad\quad\quad = 0.100 \times 4.18 \times 14.0$

  $\quad\quad\quad\quad\quad\quad\quad\quad = 5.85$ kJ

- Heat energy lost by the
  reaction $\quad\quad\quad\quad\quad\quad = -5.85$ kJ

- Moles of acid $\quad\quad\quad\quad$ = volume (in dm^3) $\times$ concentration

  (= moles of alkali) $\quad\quad \dfrac{50.0 \times 2.00}{1000} = 0.100$ mol

- Enthalpy change $\quad\quad \Delta H = \dfrac{\text{heat energy lost by the reaction}}{\text{moles of acid}}$

  $\quad\quad\quad\quad\quad\quad\quad\quad = \dfrac{-5.85}{0.100}$ kJ mol^{-1}

  $\quad\quad\quad\quad\quad\quad\quad\quad = -58.5$ kJ mol^{-1}

Examiners' Notes

The total volume of water in the reaction mixture is 100 cm^3. This has a mass of 0.10 kg. The amount of water produced by the reaction is negligibly small. The heat capacity of the solution is assumed to be the same as that of water.

Examiners' Notes

The enthalpy change is usually related to the 'moles of equation' as written. Again, this is an exothermic reaction so the sign of the enthalpy change is negative.

Essential Notes

The first law of thermodynamics is also similar to the principle of conservation of energy.

Essential Notes

The overall enthalpy change for a multi-step reaction can be calculated using the expression

$\Delta H = (\Delta H_{(\text{step 1})} + \Delta H_{(\text{step 2})} + \ldots)$
$\quad = \Sigma \Delta H_{(\text{all steps})}$

where the symbol Σ means 'sum of'.

Simple applications of Hess's law

Definition

The first law of thermodynamics states that energy can be neither created nor destroyed, but can be converted from one form into another.

Hess's law is a special case of the first law.

Definition

Hess's law states that the enthalpy change of a reaction depends only on the initial and final states of the reaction and is independent of the route by which the reaction occurs.

It follows from Hess's law that the enthalpy change of a reaction is the sum of the individual enthalpy changes of each step into which the reaction can be divided, regardless of their nature.

Hess's law is illustrated diagrammatically in Fig 1.

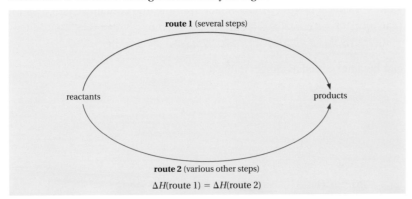

Fig 1
Hess's law in terms of a heat cycle

Hess's law can be used to determine ΔH values for reactions where direct determination is difficult. For example, the enthalpy change for any reaction can be determined if the enthalpies of combustion of the reactants and the products are known. Thus, the standard enthalpy of formation of methane can be calculated from standard enthalpies of combustion as shown in Fig 2.

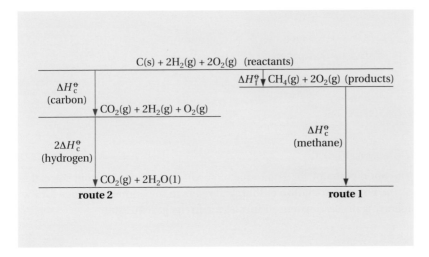

Fig 2
Using an enthalpy cycle to determine the enthalpy of formation of methane

Essential Notes

In the step where CH_4 is formed from $C(s)$ and $2H_2(g)$, the oxygen can be ignored because it is present in both the reactants and products.

Examiners' Notes

Remember $\Delta H_f^{\ominus}(O_2)$ is zero because oxygen is an element.

Examiners' Notes

In general, for any reaction
$$\Delta H^{\ominus} = \Sigma \Delta H_c^{\ominus}(\text{reactants}) - \Sigma \Delta H_c^{\ominus}(\text{products})$$

This cycle shows how an enthalpy change can be calculated from standard enthalpies of combustion. Note that in these diagrams, unlike the way equations are usually written, reactants are on one horizontal line and the products are on another.

$$\Sigma \Delta H(\text{steps in route 1}) = \Sigma \Delta H(\text{steps in route 2})$$

$$\therefore \Delta H_f^{\ominus}(\text{products}) + \Delta H_c^{\ominus}(\text{products}) = \Sigma \Delta H_c^{\ominus}(\text{reactants})$$

$$\therefore \Delta H_f^{\ominus}(\text{products}) = \Sigma \Delta H_c^{\ominus}(\text{reactants}) - \Sigma \Delta H_c^{\ominus}(\text{products})$$

$$\therefore \Delta H_f^{\ominus}(\text{methane}) = \Delta H_c^{\ominus}(\text{carbon}) + 2 \times \Delta H_c^{\ominus}(\text{hydrogen})$$
$$- \Delta H_c^{\ominus}(\text{methane})$$

$$= -393 + (2 \times -285) - (-890)$$

$$= -73 \text{ kJ mol}^{-1}$$

Enthalpy changes for reactions can also be determined from tabulated values of enthalpies of formation. For example, the enthalpy change for the reaction:

$$3CO(g) + Fe_2O_3(s) \rightarrow 2Fe(s) + 3CO_2(g)$$

can be determined as shown in Fig 3.

Fig 3
Using an enthalpy cycle to determine the enthalpy change for a reaction

Examiners' Notes

This cycle shows how an enthalpy change can be calculated from standard enthalpies of formation.

Note that $\Delta H_f^{\ominus}(Fe)$ is zero.

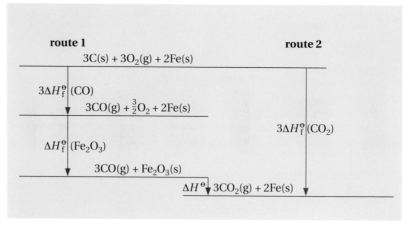

Examiners' Notes

In general for any reaction $\Delta H^{\ominus} = \Sigma \Delta H_f^{\ominus}(products) - \Sigma \Delta H_f^{\ominus}(reactants)$

Note that this expression is different from the one which involves enthalpies of combustion.

$\Sigma \Delta H(route\ 1) = \Sigma \Delta H(route\ 2)$

$\therefore \Delta H^{\ominus} + \Sigma \Delta H_f^{\ominus}(reactants) = \Sigma \Delta H_f^{\ominus}(products)$

$\therefore \Delta H^{\ominus} = \Sigma \Delta H_f^{\ominus}(products) - \Sigma \Delta H_f^{\ominus}(reactants)$

$\therefore \Delta H^{\ominus} = 3 \times \Delta H_f^{\ominus}(CO_2) - (3 \times \Delta H_f^{\ominus}(CO) + \Delta H_f^{\ominus}(Fe_2O_3))$

$= 3 \times -394 - ((3 \times -111) - 822)$

$= -27\ kJ\ mol^{-1}$

Bond enthalpies

The bond enthalpy for a diatomic molecule is also known, more correctly as the **bond dissociation enthalpy**. It refers to the enthalpy change for the following process, where all species are in the gaseous state.

$$A{-}B(g) \rightarrow A(g) + B(g) \qquad \Delta H = bond\ enthalpy$$

In polyatomic molecules it is convenient to use the term **mean bond enthalpy**.

Definition

The **mean bond enthalpy** is the average of several values of the bond dissociation enthalpy for a given type of bond, taken from a range of different compounds.

Essential Notes

Bond enthalpy calculations apply only to reactions in the gaseous state.

Consider the following processes:

$$CH_4(g) \rightarrow CH_3(g) + H(g) \qquad \Delta H = 423\ kJ\ mol^{-1}$$

$$CH_4(g) \rightarrow C(g) + 4H(g) \qquad \Delta H = 1664\ kJ\ mol^{-1}$$

The second equation involves the breaking of all four carbon–hydrogen bonds. The mean bond enthalpy can therefore be determined by dividing the value of 1664 by 4. The bond dissociation enthalpy value for breaking the H—CH_3 bond (423 kJ mol^{-1}) is slightly different from the value for the mean bond enthalpy (416 kJ mol^{-1}). The first process involves the breaking of one C—H bond and the formation of a •CH_3 radical. The second process does not involve the formation of hydrocarbon radicals; it leads only to atomic species. The mean bond enthalpy is a useful quantity when calculating reaction enthalpy changes, but its use is only approximate.

Mean bond enthalpies can be used to calculate the enthalpy change for simple reactions. The mean bond enthalpies of the reactant bonds that are broken are added together. From this value is subtracted the sum of the bond enthalpies of the product bonds that are formed. The difference is the overall enthalpy change. This is summarised in the following equation:

$$\Delta H = \Sigma(\text{mean bond enthalpy of bonds broken})$$
$$- \Sigma(\text{mean bond enthalpy of bonds formed})$$

For example, the enthalpy change for the following reaction can be calculated using the data from Table 1:

$$CH_4(g) + Cl_2(g) \rightarrow CH_3Cl(g) + HCl(g)$$

$$\Delta H = \Sigma(\text{enthalpy of bonds broken}) - \Sigma(\text{enthalpy of bonds formed})$$

$$\Delta H = (C—H + Cl—Cl) - (C—Cl + H—Cl)$$

$$= (412 + 242) - (338 + 431)$$

$$= -115 \text{ kJ mol}^{-1}$$

Table 1
Mean bond enthalpies

Bond	C—H	C—Cl	Cl—Cl	H—Cl
Mean bond enthalpy/kJ mol^{-1}	412	338	242	431

Examiners' Notes

The mean bond enthalpy per C—H bond is $\dfrac{1664}{4}$

= 416 kJ mol^{-1}.

In data books, the mean bond enthalpy refers to the average of the bond enthalpy values for many different compounds.

Examiners' Notes

This calculation assumes that the C—H bond enthalpy in CH_3Cl is equal to that in CH_4; this is a good approximation.

Examiners' Notes

It is not always necessary to consider all the bonds in the reactants and products. In this example, the answer can be determined by considering only the bonds broken and those formed.

3.2.2 Kinetics

Collision theory

When two substances react, particles (molecules, atoms or ions) of one substance must collide with particles of the other. However, not all collisions result in a reaction; i.e. not all collisions are productive. This situation arises because particles will react only when they collide with sufficient energy. The minimum energy necessary for reaction is known as the **activation energy** (See also Section 3.2.3).

Essential Notes

In addition, before a reaction can occur, it is often necessary for the orientation of molecules to be correct on collision.

Maxwell–Boltzmann distribution

In a sample of gas or liquid, the molecules are in constant motion and collide both with each other and with the walls of their container. Such collisions are said to be **elastic**; i.e. no energy is lost during the collision, but energy can be transferred from one molecule to another.

Consequently, at a given temperature, molecules in a particular sample will have a spread of energies about the most probable energy. James Clark Maxwell and Ludwig Boltzmann derived a theory from which it is possible to draw curves showing how these energies are distributed. A plot of the number of molecules with a particular energy against that energy (see Fig 4) is known as the Maxwell–Boltzmann distribution curve.

Fig 4
Distribution of energies at a particular temperature

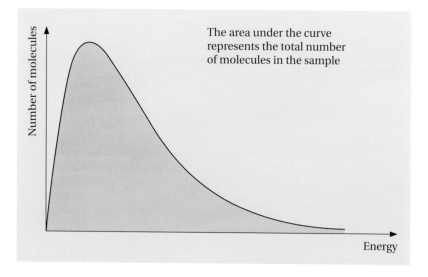

The area under the curve represents the total number of molecules in the sample

This distribution curve has several important features. There are no molecules with zero energy and only a few with very high energies. There is also no maximum energy for molecules – the curve in Fig 4 approaches zero **asymptotically** at high energy. The most probable energy of a molecule corresponds to the maximum of the curve as indicated in Fig 5.

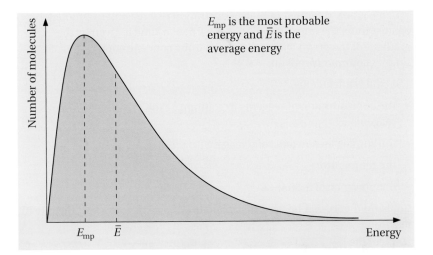

Fig 5
Most probable and average energies

E_{mp} is the most probable energy and $\bar{E}$ is the average energy

Effect of temperature variation on the Maxwell–Boltzmann curve

If the temperature of the sample is increased from T_1 to T_2, the average energy of the molecules increases, and the most probable energy of the molecules increases. The spread of energies also increases and the shape of the distribution curve changes as shown in Fig 6. For a fixed sample of gas, the total number of molecules is unchanged so the area under the curve remains constant (see also section 3.2.3).

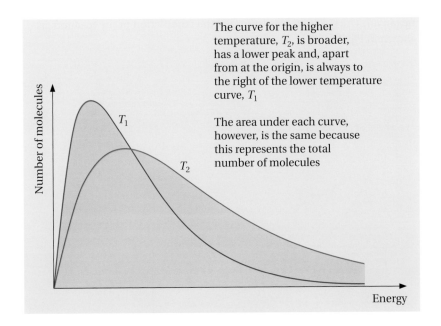

Fig 6
Distribution of energies at two temperatures

The curve for the higher temperature, T_2, is broader, has a lower peak and, apart from at the origin, is always to the right of the lower temperature curve, T_1

The area under each curve, however, is the same because this represents the total number of molecules

Factors affecting reaction rate

> ### Definition
> The **rate of a reaction is** defined as the change in concentration of a substance in unit time.

When a graph is plotted of the concentration of a reagent or product against time, the rate of reaction at a particular time is given by the gradient of the graph at that time, with units concentration time^{-1}–commonly $\text{mol dm}^{-3}\,\text{s}^{-1}$.

The rate is affected by:

- the concentration of reagents in solution or the pressure of gaseous reagents
- the surface area of any solid reagent
- the temperature
- the presence of a catalyst.

Collision theory can be used to explain how these factors affect the rate of reaction.

Concentration

Increasing the concentration of a reagent increases the number of particles in a given volume and so increases the collision rate, and hence the chance of productive collisions. This change increases the rate of reaction (if the reagent appears in the rate equation – see *Collins Student Support Materials: Unit 4 – Kinetics, Equilibria and Organic Chemistry, section 3.4.1*).

As a reaction proceeds, reagents are used up, so their concentrations fall. The rate is therefore at its greatest at the start of a reaction. On a concentration–time graph, the initial gradient is the steepest (most negative). The gradient falls to zero at the completion of the reaction, as shown in Fig 7.

Fig 7
Fall in concentration of reagent with time at constant temperature

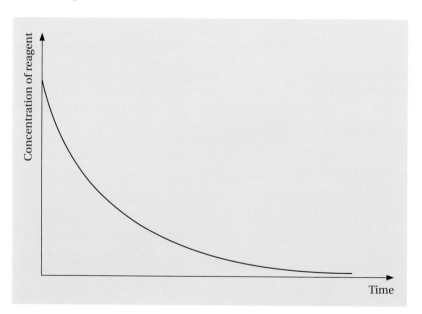

Surface area

When one reagent is a solid, the rate of its reaction with a gas or with a substance in solution is increased if the solid is broken into smaller pieces. This process increases the surface area of the solid and allows more

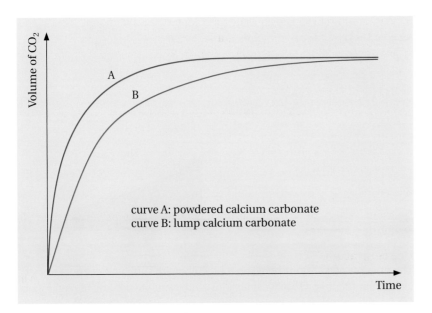

Fig 8
Volume of CO_2 against time at constant temperature

curve A: powdered calcium carbonate
curve B: lump calcium carbonate

collisions to occur with particles of the other reagent. For example, when a given mass of calcium carbonate is reacted with an excess of hydrochloric acid and the volume of carbon dioxide produced is plotted against time, the initial gradient of the graph is much steeper when powdered carbonate is used (Fig 8, curve A) than when lumps are reacted (Fig 8, curve B).

Note that the same amount of calcium carbonate must have been used up in each experiment since the final volume of CO_2 is the same in both cases.

When an ionic solid is dissolved in a solvent, its particles are completely separated so that the rate is increased even further, and the reaction may become almost instantaneous. Precipitates form as soon as the correct solutions are mixed, since the free ions in solution can easily collide and react.

Temperature

An increase in temperature always increases the rate of a reaction. According to kinetic theory, the mean kinetic energy of particles is proportional to the temperature. At higher temperatures, particles move more quickly (they have more energy) and there are more collisions in a given time.

More important, however, is the fact that particles will react only if, on collision, they have at least the minimum amount of energy, which is known as the activation energy.

> **Definition**
> The **activation energy** of a reaction is the minimum energy required for reaction to occur.

At higher temperatures, the mean energy of the particles is increased. The Maxwell–Boltzmann curves in Fig 9 show that, if the activation energy for a reaction is E_a, the number of molecules with energy greater than E_a (as shown by the shaded area) is much greater at temperature T_2 than at the lower temperature T_1.

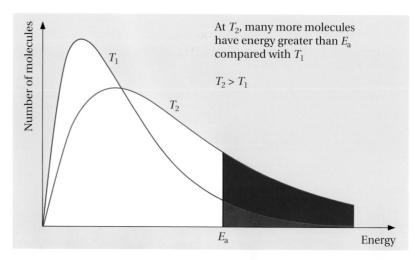

Fig 9
Molecules with energy greater than E_a at different temperatures

At T_2, many more molecules have energy greater than E_a compared with T_1

$T_2 > T_1$

Examiners' Notes

E_a does not change with temperature, but the number of molecules with a greater energy than this does.

The number of collisions between molecules with sufficient energy to react, i.e. the number of productive collisions, and therefore the rate of reaction, is very much greater at the higher temperature. Consequently, small temperature increases can lead to large increases in rate, as shown in Fig 10.

Fig 10
Change of rate as temperature rises

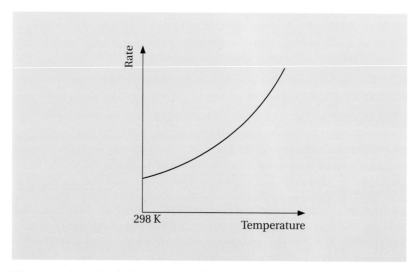

Many reactions – including several which are very exothermic – do not occur because the activation energy required is too high. For example, petrol reacts with oxygen in air in a very exothermic reaction, but a petrol–air mixture exists in the petrol tank of a car and will react only if sparked.

Catalysts

Examiners' Notes

An example of a negative catalyst, i.e. one which slows down a reaction, is antimony oxide, which is used as a flame retardant in plastics such as PVC.

A **catalyst** is a substance which alters the rate of a reaction without itself being consumed during the reaction. Most of the catalysts used are positive catalysts: they increase the rate of reaction.

A positive catalyst operates by providing an alternative route or reaction mechanism which has a lower activation energy E_{cat} than the uncatalysed route. Fig 11 shows a reaction profile for a catalysed and an uncatalysed reaction. Note that the catalyst has no effect on the overall enthalpy change for the reaction. The catalyst also has no effect on the equilibrium position since this depends only on the relative energies of the reactants and products.

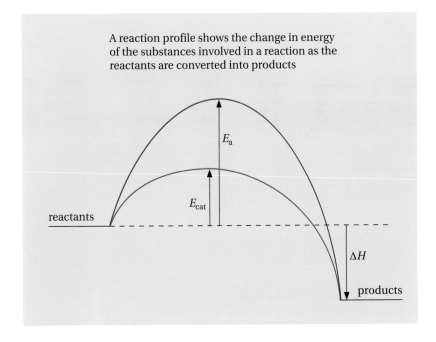

A reaction profile shows the change in energy of the substances involved in a reaction as the reactants are converted into products

Fig 11
Reaction profile showing an uncatalysed and a one-step catalysed reaction

The reaction profile in Fig 11 shows a one-step catalysed reaction. In many cases the catalysed reaction occurs in more than one step and a double-humped reaction profile will be seen, as in Fig 12.

Essential Notes

Catalytic action is covered in *Collins Student Support Materials: Unit 5 – Energetics, Redox and Inorganic Chemistry*, section 3.5.4.

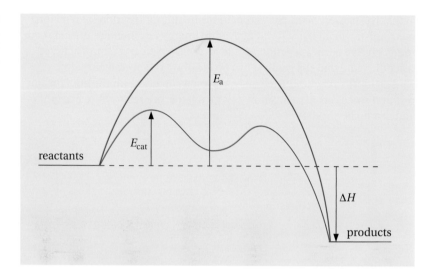

Fig 12
Reaction profile showing an uncatalysed and a two-step catalysed reaction

The Maxwell–Boltzmann curve in Fig 13 shows that a catalyst which lowers the activation energy from E_a to E_{cat} will produce many more molecules (the shaded area) that are able to react. In the presence of a catalyst, therefore, the rate is increased.

Fig 13
Effect of a catalyst on activation energies

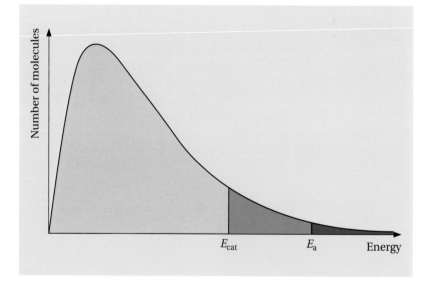

3.2.3 Equilibria

Dynamic nature of equilibrium

Many chemical reactions continue until one of the reactants is completely used up, and then reaction stops. Such reactions are said to **go to completion**. The reaction between magnesium and oxygen is a good example of a reaction that goes to completion:

$$2Mg + O_2 \rightarrow 2MgO$$

Many other reactions, however, do not go to completion and are **reversible**. When the reactants and products have different colours, it is easy to demonstrate the reversibility of the reaction. For example, when dilute sulfuric acid is added to an aqueous solution containing yellow chromate(VI) ions, the following reaction occurs, forming orange dichromate(VI) ions:

$$2CrO_4{}^{2-} + 2H^+ \rightarrow Cr_2O_7{}^{2-} + H_2O$$

(yellow)　　　　　　　　(orange)

If an aqueous solution of sodium hydroxide is now added to the orange solution, the reaction is reversed and yellow chromate(VI) ions are re-formed:

$$Cr_2O_7{}^{2-} + 2OH^- \rightarrow 2CrO_4{}^{2-} + H_2O$$

(orange)　　　　　　　　(yellow)

The overall reaction can be represented by the equation:

$$2CrO_4{}^{2-} + 2H^+ \rightleftharpoons Cr_2O_7{}^{2-} + H_2O$$

(yellow)　　　　　　　(orange)

The $\rightleftharpoons$ sign is used to indicate that the reaction is reversible. By convention, the reaction shown as occurring from left to right in the equation is called the **forward reaction** and the reaction occurring in the opposite direction is called the **backward reaction** or the **reverse reaction**. Since the reaction still continues in both directions, it is said to be **dynamic**. When both reactions occur at the same rate, the concentrations of the chromate(VI) and dichromate(VI) ions remain constant, and a **chemical equilibrium** has been established. A chemical equilibrium can only be established if reagents are neither added to, nor taken from, the reaction mixture.

> **Examiners' Notes**
>
> Other reactions which can be used in the laboratory to illustrate the reversibility of reactions include $[Co(H_2O)_6]^{2+}$ with $Cl^-(aq)$ and $Fe^{3+}(aq)$ with $SCN^-(aq)$.

When a chemical equilibrium is established:

- reactants and products are present at all times
- the reaction is dynamic, i.e. it proceeds in both directions
- the concentrations of reactants and products remain constant.

If reactants are added or if products are removed, the equilibrium is displaced.

Effects of changing reaction conditions

The effect on the equilibrium position of the following is considered below:

- change in concentration
- change in pressure
- change in temperature
- addition of a catalyst.

For most reactions the qualitative effect of changing reaction conditions can be predicted using **Le Chatelier's principle**.

> **Definition**
>
> *Le Chatelier's principle states that a system at equilibrium will respond to oppose any change imposed upon it.*

Effect of a change in concentration

If all other conditions remain the same and the concentration of any of the species involved in an equilibrium reaction is changed, then the concentrations of the other species must also change. Le Chatelier's principle can be used to deduce the changes that occur. For example, if the concentration of a reactant is increased, or the concentration of a product is decreased (e.g. by removing some of it), the position of equilibrium moves to the right and more product is formed.

Consider the reaction:

$$CH_3COOC_2H_5(l) + H_2O(l) \rightleftharpoons CH_3COOH(l) + C_2H_5OH(l)$$

If a little more water or $CH_3COOC_2H_5(l)$ is added, some of the additional reagent reacts and the equilibrium position is displaced to the right. As a result, the equilibrium yields of $CH_3COOH(l)$ and $C_2H_5OH(l)$ are both increased. Similarly, if more $CH_3COOH(l)$ or more $C_2H_5OH(l)$ is added, the equilibrium is displaced to the left and the equilibrium mixture will contain more $CH_3COOC_2H_5(l)$ and $H_2O(l)$.

Effect of a change in total pressure

Changes in total pressure have a significant effect on the composition of a mixture at equilibrium only if the reaction involves gases. The changes observed are due to changes in the concentrations of the species present. An increase in total pressure, according to Le Chatelier's principle, will displace the equilibrium in a direction that tries to reduce the increased pressure – the system responds by decreasing the number of moles of gas present, thus lowering the total pressure. The converse of this statement also applies.

For example, consider the reaction:

$$CH_4(g) + H_2O(g) \rightleftharpoons 3H_2(g) + CO(g)$$

In this equation, the total number of moles of gaseous reactants is two – i.e. 1 mol of $CH_4(g)$ plus 1 mol of $H_2O(g)$, and the total number of moles of gaseous products is four – i.e. 3 mol of $H_2(g)$ plus 1 mol of $CO(g)$.

Thus, at a given temperature, the equilibrium amount of products can be increased by *reducing* the total pressure, so that the system responds by moving to the right to produce a greater number of moles of gas, in an attempt to increase the pressure.

Effect of a change in temperature

A change in temperature alters the rate of both the forward and the backward reactions. These are changed by different amounts, so the position of the equilibrium is altered. The simple rule which says that a system at equilibrium will react to oppose any change imposed upon it (Le Chatelier's principle) can be used to predict the effects of a change in temperature.

An increase in temperature is opposed by a movement of the position of equilibrium, either to the left or to the right, in order to absorb the added heat energy. Heat energy is absorbed by moving in the **endothermic** direction.

A decrease in temperature is opposed by a movement of the position of equilibrium, either to the left or to the right, in order to gain the lost heat energy. Heat energy is gained by moving in the **exothermic** direction.

In an **exothermic reaction** heat energy is evolved. An increase in temperature requires removal of the added heat energy by an equilibrium shift in the endothermic direction. The equilibrium position is displaced to the left and the equilibrium mixture contains a lower concentration of products. It is important to note, however, that although the new equilibrium mixture obtained at a higher temperature contains less product, the time taken to reach this new equilibrium is reduced because of the increased rate of the reaction.

For example, consider the effect of a change in temperature on the exothermic reaction:

$$H_2(g) + I_2(g) \rightleftharpoons 2HI(g) \qquad \Delta H = -9.6 \text{ kJ mol}^{-1}$$

At 298 K, this equilibrium lies far to the right and the reaction mixture at equilibrium contains a high percentage of HI(g). If the temperature rises, the percentage of HI(g) present in the equilibrium mixture falls.

In an **endothermic reaction** heat energy is absorbed. An increase in temperature requires replacement of the lost heat energy, once again by an equilibrium shift in the endothermic direction. In this case, the equilibrium position is displaced to the right and the equilibrium mixture contains a higher concentration of products. Thus, for an endothermic reaction, an increase in temperature increases the equilibrium concentration of products.

Consider, for example, the endothermic reaction:

$$N_2(g) + O_2(g) \rightleftharpoons 2NO(g) \qquad \Delta H = 180 \text{ kJ mol}^{-1}$$

At 298 K, the equilibrium lies so far to the left that the equilibrium mixture contains almost no NO(g). Increasing the temperature to 1500 K does increase the equilibrium yield of NO(g), but this is still too small for the direct combination of nitrogen and oxygen to be an economically viable method of preparing NO(g).

Essential Notes

If pressure is lowered, the rate of the reaction decreases.

Essential Notes

The opposite is true if the temperature is *decreased*.

Essential Notes

The converse is true if the temperature is *decreased*.

Essential Notes

Changes in pressure have no effect on the position of this equilibrium since the number of moles of gas on each side of the equation is the same.

The effects of changes in temperature on equilibria can be summarised as follows: an *increase* in temperature always displaces the equilibrium in the *endothermic* direction.

Table 2
Effects of temperature changes on equilibria

Reaction enthalpy	Change in temperature	Displacement of equilibrium	Yield of product	Rate of attainment of equilibrium
exothermic	increased	to the left	reduced	increased
exothermic	decreased	to the right	increased	reduced
endothermic	increased	to the right	increased	increased
endothermic	decreased	to the left	reduced	reduced

Effect of a catalyst

The addition of a catalyst to a mixture at equilibrium has no effect on the composition of the equilibrium mixture. This is because a catalyst causes an equal increase in the rates of both the forward and the backward reactions which themselves are equal at equilibrium. Hence, the equilibrium position is achieved more quickly, but the composition of the equilibrium mixture is unchanged.

Importance of equilibria in industrial processes

Many chemicals are manufactured on a large scale. The processes used are designed to give the optimum yield. All the factors which affect the position of a particular equilibrium reaction must be carefully considered.

Ethanol and methanol are important organic compounds which are increasingly being used as fuels. Both of these alcohols are manufactured on a large scale.

Ethanol production

Ethanol is produced industrially by the hydration of ethene:

$$C_2H_4(g) + H_2O(g) \rightleftharpoons C_2H_5OH(g) \quad \Delta H = -46 \text{ kJ mol}^{-1}$$

Essential Notes

Ethanol is also produced industrially by fermentation; this process is considered in section 3.2.10.

The hydration of ethene is an exothermic reaction. Application of Le Chatelier's principle predicts that this reaction will be opposed by an increase in temperature, so that the best equilibrium yield of ethanol will be obtained at low temperatures. However, at low temperatures the rate of reaction is slow and, although a high equilibrium yield can be achieved, it may take a long time to reach equilibrium. Increasing the temperature speeds up the rate of attainment of equilibrium, but reduces the equilibrium yield. A compromise between yield and speed of reaction is clearly necessary and a typical operating temperature for this reaction is around 300 °C.

The equation above shows that 2 mol of gaseous reactants (one of ethene and one of water) form 1 mol of gaseous product (ethanol). Application of Le Chatelier's principle predicts that the hydration of ethene will be favoured by a high pressure. The pressure used is a compromise between the cost of generating high pressure and the additional value of the increased equilibrium yield. A typical pressure for this reaction is 6.5 MPa.

The acid H_3PO_4 is used as a catalyst for this reaction. This catalyst increases the rate of both the forward and backward reactions to the same extent. Hence, the time taken to reach equilibrium is reduced, but the equilibrium yield of ethanol is unaltered.

Methanol production

Methanol is produced industrially by the reaction between carbon monoxide and hydrogen:

$$CO(g) + 2H_2(g) \rightleftharpoons CH_3OH(g) \qquad \Delta H = -90 \text{ kJ mol}^{-1}$$

This equation shows that 3 mol of gaseous reactants form 1 mol of gaseous product. Application of Le Chatelier's principle predicts that a high equilibrium yield will be obtained at high pressure. Again, the cost of generating the high pressure must be balanced against the value of the increased equilibrium yield of methanol. A typical pressure used in industry is around 5 MPa.

Since the reaction between carbon monoxide and hydrogen is exothermic, application of Le Chatelier's principle predicts that a high equilibrium yield of methanol will be obtained at a low temperature. However, as the rate of the reaction will be low at a relatively low temperature, a compromise is again required and a typical operating temperature is around 400 °C.

The time required for the reaction to reach equilibrium is reduced by the use of a catalyst: a mixture of chromium(III) oxide, Cr_2O_3, and zinc oxide, ZnO, is often used as the catalyst for this reaction.

Ethanol and methanol as liquid fuels

Both methanol and ethanol can be mixed with petrol to produce fuels for internal combustion engines.

Ethanol is of increasing importance as a constituent of motor car fuels Most spark–ignited petrol engines will operate efficiently with petrol–ethanol blends containing up to 10% ethanol.

Methanol is not as flammable as petrol. Some vehicles, including 'drag racers', use methanol as their main fuel source and methanol has also been used to fuel Indianapolis 500 race cars.

Examiners' Notes

The anhydrous ethanol used in petrol–ethanol blends must not contain more than 1% water.

Examiners' Notes

Modern flexible-fuel vehicles (FFVs) are designed to use petrol–ethanol blends containing up to 85% ethanol.

3.2.4 Redox reactions

Oxidation and reduction

The term **redox** is used for reactions which involve both **reduction** and **oxidation**. Originally the term oxidation was applied to the formation of a metal oxide when a metal reacted with oxygen. For example:

$$2Mg + O_2 \rightarrow 2MgO$$

The reverse of this reaction was given the name reduction, and reducing agents were substances which removed oxygen. Hence, in the reaction:

$$Fe_2O_3 + 2Al \rightarrow Al_2O_3 + 2Fe$$

aluminium behaves as a reducing agent. In the reaction:

$$CuO + C \rightarrow Cu + CO$$

carbon is the reducing agent.

The role of hydrogen as a reducing agent is also recognised in the following definition:

- oxidation – the addition of oxygen (or the removal of hydrogen)
- reduction – the removal of oxygen (or the addition of hydrogen).

Now consider the reactions:

$$SO_2 + H_2O + HgO \rightarrow H_2SO_4 + Hg$$

$$SO_2 + 2H_2O + Cl_2 \rightarrow H_2SO_4 + 2HCl$$

In the first case, HgO, by losing oxygen to form Hg, has clearly acted as the oxidising agent. In the second case, since oxidation of $SO_2(aq)$ to $SO_3(aq)$ has again occurred, the oxidising agent must be chlorine. To understand why chlorine is able to act as an oxidising agent we need to introduce the concept of oxidation state and redefine what we mean by the terms **oxidation** and **reduction**.

Oxidation states

Examiners' Notes

Oxidation state can also be called oxidation number.

For a simple ion, the oxidation state is the charge on the ion:

Na^+, K^+, Ag^+	have an oxidation state of	$+1$
$Mg^{2+}, Ca^{2+}, Ba^{2+}$	have an oxidation state of	$+2$
F^-, Cl^-, I^-	have an oxidation state of	-1
O^{2-}, S^{2-}	have an oxidation state of	-2

The **oxidation state** of the central atom in a complex ion (an ion consisting of several atoms) is the charge it would have if it existed as a solitary

Table 3
Data for assignment of oxidation states

Essential Notes

For combined oxygen in peroxides, each oxygen has an oxidation state of -1.

Species	Oxidation state
elements not combined with others	0
oxygen in compounds, except peroxides	-2
hydrogen in compounds, except in metal hydrides	$+1$
hydrogen in metal hydrides	-1
Group 1 metals in compounds	$+1$
Group 2 metals in compounds	$+2$

simple ion without bonds to other species. Table 3 gives some data which can be used to establish the oxidation state of an atom in a complex ion.

Calculation of the oxidation state of a combined element in an oxo-ion

Using the data given in Table 3, the oxidation state of an atom in a complex ion can be calculated. The principles used are that the sum of the oxidation states in a neutral compound is zero and that the sum of the oxidation states in an ion is equal to the overall charge of the ion. For example, the oxidation state of phosphorus in PO_4^{3-} is determined as follows.

The overall charge is -3, therefore:

oxidation state of phosphorus + (4 × oxidation state of oxygen) = -3

Hence: oxidation state of phosphorus $- 8 = -3$

Thus: oxidation state of phosphorus $= +5$

Some more examples of oxo-ion complexes are given in Table 4.

Species	Number of oxygen atoms	Total oxidation number due to oxygen	Overall charge on the ion	Oxidation state of central atom	Name of species
SO_4^{2-}	4	-8	-2	$+6$	sulfate
NO_3^{-}	3	-6	-1	$+5$	nitrate
ClO_3^{-}	3	-6	-1	$+5$	chlorate(V)
ClO^{-}	1	-2	-1	$+1$	chlorate(I)

Table 4
Calculation of the oxidation state of some central atoms in oxo-ions

Redox equations

Redox reactions can be summarised as shown:

Definitions

Oxidation is the process of electron loss. Oxidising agents are electron acceptors.

Reduction is the process of electron gain. Reducing agents are electron donors.

Identifying redox reactions

Redox reactions can readily be understood by the use of these definitions of oxidation and reduction.

In the reaction:

$Fe_2O_3 + 2Al \rightarrow Al_2O_3 + 2Fe$

Examiners' Notes

The sum of the oxidation states of all the atoms in any complex is equal to the overall charge of that species.

Examiners' Notes

The ending 'ate' means that the ion has a negative charge.

Examiners' Notes

More precisely, SO_4^{2-} should be called sulfate(VI) and NO_3^{-} should be called nitrate(V) but these oxidation states are omitted in common usage.

Examiners' Notes

The mnemonic O I L R I G, which stands for Oxidation Is Loss, Reduction Is Gain, is a useful aid when learning how electrons are transferred in a redox reaction.

Essential Notes

Half-equations are discussed more fully on p 25.

the changes which occur are shown in the following half-equations:

$$Fe^{3+} + 3e^- \rightarrow Fe$$

$$Al \rightarrow Al^{3+} + 3e^-$$

The oxidation state of iron changes from $+3$ in Fe_2O_3 to zero in the uncombined metal, i.e. a reduction occurs. The oxidation state of aluminium changes from zero in the uncombined metal to $+3$ in Al_2O_3 and the aluminium metal is oxidised.

Equally, in the oxidation by chlorine of $SO_2(aq)$ to $SO_3(aq)$, i.e. $H_2SO_4(aq)$:

$$Cl_2 + SO_2 + 2H_2O \rightarrow H_2SO_4 + 2HCl$$

chlorine is reduced from oxidation state zero to oxidation state -1, as shown by the following half-equation:

$$Cl_2 + 2e^- \rightarrow 2Cl^-$$

The oxidation state of sulfur is increased from $+4$ to $+6$ by oxidation:

$$SO_2 + 2H_2O \rightarrow H_2SO_4 + 2H^+ + 2e^-$$

Example

Explain why the following is a redox reaction:

$$Mg + 2HCl \rightarrow MgCl_2 + H_2$$

Answer

In this reaction, the oxidation state of hydrogen, combined in hydrochloric acid, changes from $+1$ to zero in the uncombined element; i.e. the hydrogen ion is reduced by the magnesium metal. The uncombined magnesium metal, in oxidation state zero, is changed into combined magnesium in magnesium chloride, with an oxidation state of $+2$. Thus, the magnesium metal is oxidised by the hydrochloric acid.

The use of an ionic equation makes this redox reaction easy to recognise:

$$Mg + 2H^+ \rightarrow Mg^{2+} + H_2$$

Example

Explain why the following is a redox reaction:

$$MnO_2 + 4HCl \rightarrow MnCl_2 + Cl_2 + 2H_2O$$

Answer

Deductions using the oxidation states of combined oxygen and chlorine show that, in this reaction, manganese is reduced from oxidation state $+4$ to $+2$ by the chloride ions in hydrochloric acid. Some of the chlorine, combined in HCl, is converted into the uncombined element chlorine. This change, from oxidation state -1 to zero, is due to oxidation by manganese(IV) oxide. This simple ionic equation shows the changes in oxidation state:

$$Mn^{4+} + 2Cl^- \rightarrow Mn^{2+} + Cl_2$$

Example

Explain why the following is not a redox reaction:

$$MgO + 2HCl \rightarrow MgCl_2 + H_2O$$

Answer

At an initial glance this might appear to be a redox reaction as the magnesium oxide 'loses' oxygen. There is, however, no change in the oxidation state of any of the elements present. The reaction is that of an acid with a base, resulting in the formation of a salt and water.

$$MgO + 2H^+ \rightarrow Mg^{2+} + H_2O$$

Half-equations for redox reactions

Earlier in this section the equations:

$$Fe^{3+} + 3e^- \rightarrow Fe$$
$$Al \rightarrow Al^{3+} + 3e^-$$

were given. These are examples of half-equations. The overall equation for a redox reaction can be separated into two half-equations; one shows reduction, the other oxidation. In each case the half-equation is balanced using electrons, so that the overall charge on both sides of the half-equation is the same.

These equations are often much simpler than molecular equations because they only show the actual species involved in the reaction. It is only necessary to know the initial and final species in a redox reaction to be able to construct half-equations for both processes.

Construction of half-equations for reactions

When constructing any half-equation, the following points must be observed:

- only *one* element in a half-equation changes oxidation state
- the half-equation must balance for atoms
- the half-equation must balance for charge.

When constructing a half-equation for reactions occurring in aqueous solution, water provides a source of oxygen and any 'surplus' oxygen is converted into water by reaction with hydrogen ions from an acid.

By applying these rules, half-equations for the reduction of any species can be deduced.

Example

Deduce the half-equation for the reduction, in acid solution, of NO_3^- to NO.

Answer

The oxidation state of nitrogen changes from $+5$ in NO_3^- to $+2$ in NO and nitrogen is reduced. The oxidation state of the oxygen is still -2, but two of the three oxygens combine with four hydrogen ions (provided by the added acid) to form two water molecules:

$$NO_3^- + 4H^+ \rightarrow NO + 2H_2O$$

This incomplete half-equation now balances for atoms but not for charge, with a total charge of $+3$ on the left-hand side and zero on the right-hand side. Three electrons must be added to the left-hand side to give the balanced half-equation:

$$NO_3^- + 4H^+ + 3e^- \rightarrow NO + 2H_2O$$

Construction of overall equations for redox reactions

The overall equation for any redox reaction can be obtained by adding together two half-equations, making sure that the number of electrons given by the reducing agent exactly balances the number of electrons accepted by the oxidising agent.

Example

When chlorine gas is bubbled through an aqueous solution of potassium bromide, the solution turns yellow as bromide ions are oxidised to bromine by chlorine, which is itself reduced to chloride ions. Write half-equations for the oxidation of bromide ions and for the reduction of chlorine, and use these to deduce an overall equation for the reaction.

Answer

The half-equation for the reduction of chlorine is:

$$Cl_2 + 2e^- \rightarrow 2Cl^-$$

The half-equation for the oxidation of bromide ions to bromine is:

$$2Br^- \rightarrow Br_2 + 2e^-$$

The number of electrons gained by chlorine in the first equation must equal the number of electrons given by two bromide ions in the second equation. The overall equation can therefore be obtained by simply adding together the two half-equations. The overall equation does not involve electrons, because they cancel out:

$$Cl_2 + 2e^- \rightarrow 2Cl^-$$
$$2Br^- \rightarrow Br_2 + 2e^-$$
$$\overline{Cl_2 + 2Br^- \rightarrow 2Cl^- + Br_2}$$

Examiners' Notes

Potassium ions take no part in this reaction and can be omitted from the equations. They are called spectator ions.

Example

When concentrated nitric acid is added to copper metal, copper is oxidised to oxidation state +2 and nitric acid is reduced to nitrogen(IV) oxide. Write half-equations for the oxidation of copper and for the reduction of nitric acid, and use these to deduce an overall equation for the reaction.

Answer

The following half-equation for copper shows that uncombined copper metal is oxidised by loss of electrons:

$$Cu \rightarrow Cu^{2+} + 2e^-$$

The reduction reaction involves the reduction of nitrogen from +5 in HNO_3 to +4 in NO_2:

$$HNO_3 + H^+ + e^- \rightarrow NO_2 + H_2O$$

It is necessary to add H^+ ions to the left-hand side of this half-equation to combine with the 'surplus' oxygen (see page 25).

The two half-equations can now be combined to give an overall redox equation for the reaction. When this is done, the number of electrons required by the species being reduced and the number given by the species being oxidised must be the same, so that the equation for the overall redox reaction does not contain electrons.

In this example, the half-equation for the reduction of nitric acid must be doubled, so that the overall equation will correctly show that the two electrons lost by copper metal are accepted by nitric acid.

The overall equation for the reaction is given by addition:

$$Cu \rightarrow Cu^{2+} + 2e^-$$
$$2HNO_3 + 2H^+ + 2e^- \rightarrow 2NO_2 + 2H_2O$$
$$\overline{2HNO_3 + 2H^+ + Cu \rightarrow Cu^{2+} + 2NO_2 + 2H_2O}$$

Essential Notes

Other useful examples include the reduction of concentrated H_2SO_4 to SO_2, S or H_2S when warmed with solid NaI (see section 3.2.5).

In certain cases, where the same species appears on both sides of an overall equation obtained by the addition of two half-equations, it is necessary to cancel such a species so that it only appears on one side of the final equation. Water molecules and hydrogen ions are the most common species which need to be treated in this way. Ions which take no part in the reaction are also omitted.

3.2.5 Group 7, the halogens

The halogens form a family of non-metallic elements which show clear similarities and well-defined trends in their properties as the relative atomic mass increases.

Trends in physical properties

It is not necessary to remember the data, but it is necessary to know and be able to explain the observed trends. Some data are given in Table 5.

Table 5
Group 7 data

Element	Atomic number	Outer electrons	Atomic radius/nm	Radius of X^- ion/ nm	Boiling point/K	Electro-negativity
F	9	$2s^2 2p^5$	0.071	0.133	85	4.0
Cl	17	$3s^2 3p^5$	0.099	0.180	238	3.0
Br	35	$4s^2 4p^5$	0.114	0.195	332	2.8
I	53	$5s^2 5p^5$	0.133	0.215	457	2.5

Trend in electronegativity of the halogens

The term electronegativity was introduced in *Collins Student Support Materials: Unit 1 – Foundation Chemistry*, section 3.1.3. **Electronegativity** is the power of an atom to attract electron density in a covalent bond. The data show that the electronegativity of the halogens decreases as the atomic number increases.

To explain this trend, three important factors must be considered:

- the **atomic number**, which gives the nuclear charge. As this increases, the attraction for the bonding electron pair in a covalent bond might be expected to increase.

- the number of **electron shells**, which is indicated by the outer electron configuration of the atom. As this number increases, the shielding of the outer electrons from attraction by the nucleus increases. This results in the outer electrons being less strongly attracted.

- the **atomic radius** of the atom. The attraction between oppositely charged particles falls rapidly as the distance between them increases. As the radius of the atom increases, the outer electrons are further from the nucleus, which therefore attracts them less strongly.

The electronegativity of an element depends on a balance between these three factors. The changes in the values of electronegativity given for the halogens show that the increase in shielding and the increase in atomic radius more than compensate for the increase in nuclear charge.

The large electronegativity value for fluorine means that the bond between an element and fluorine is likely to be more polar than the bond formed between the same element and the other halogens.

Trend in boiling point of the halogens

All halogens exist as diatomic molecules, X_2. The attraction between these molecules in the liquid state is due to weak intermolecular forces called van der Waals' forces (see *Collins Student Support Materials: Unit 1 – Foundation Chemistry*, section 3.1.3). These are caused by temporary fluctuations in electron density within the molecules, resulting in temporary dipole attractions between the molecules.

The magnitude of van der Waals' attractive forces increases with the size of the molecules. This fact explains why, as both atomic and molecular radii of the halogens increase with increasing atomic number, the boiling points of the halogens also increase, as shown by the data in Table 5.

Trends in chemical properties

Oxidising power of the halogens

When any reagent is oxidised, electrons are taken from it. The electrons are accepted by the oxidising agent, which is itself reduced. The trend in oxidising power of the halogens is characterised by a decrease from strongly-oxidising fluorine to weakly-oxidising iodine.

The reasons for the decreasing trend in oxidising power from fluorine to iodine down Group 7 are quite complex, in that they involve an overall balance of energies in the following process:

$$\tfrac{1}{2}X_2 + e^- \rightarrow X^-$$

It is helpful to consider this process as occurring in three stages:

- the strength of the X—X bond (breaking to form X atoms in the gaseous phase)

- the affinity of an X atom for an electron (forming an X^- ion in the gaseous phase)

- the energy released when the X^- ion goes into solution or into a crystal lattice.

These three features affect the halogens differently:

- the very strong oxidising ability of the fluorine molecule can be attributed partly to the weakness of the F—F bond

- the electron affinity does not vary greatly from one halogen atom to the next, so has little effect on the relative oxidising power

- the fluoride ion, being the smallest, has the most to gain from being hydrated or entering a crystal, whereas the iodide ion, being the largest, benefits much less.

Thus, the trend is a decrease in oxidising power from fluorine to iodine:

$$F_2 > Cl_2 > Br_2 > I_2$$

The relative oxidising power of chlorine, bromine and iodine can be determined experimentally in the laboratory by a series of displacement reactions. In these experiments, aqueous solutions of the three halogens are added separately to aqueous solutions containing the other two halide ions. The results are given in Tables 6–8.

Examiners' Notes

Fluorine is the strongest of all oxidising agents.

Examiners' Notes

The energy released when the X^- ion goes into solution or becomes part of an ionic lattice decreases as the size of the ion increases, being largest for the small F^- ion and least for the big I^- ion.

Examiners' Notes

The F—F bond is weak because of repulsion between non-bonding electron pairs on the two atoms. The electron pairs are close together because the F atoms are small.

Essential Notes

Sea water contains a low concentration of bromide ions. Bromine is extracted from it by treating the sea water with chlorine. The liberated bromine is expelled from the water using air, and is then concentrated in a series of separate stages.

Table 6
The reactions of $Cl_2(aq)$ with $Br^-(aq)$ and $I^-(aq)$

Halide	Observations	Conclusion	Equation
Br^-(aq)	yellow/brown solution	Br_2 displaced	$2Br^- + Cl_2 \rightarrow 2Cl^- + Br_2$
I^-(aq)	brown solution and/or black precipitate	I_2 displaced	$2I^- + Cl_2 \rightarrow 2Cl^- + I_2$

Essential Notes

Iodine is almost insoluble in water, but in the presence of iodide ions it dissolves to form the complex ion I_3^-(aq) which is brown.

Table 7
The reactions of $Br_2(aq)$ with $Cl^-(aq)$ and $I^-(aq)$

Halide	Observations	Conclusion	Equation
Cl^-(aq)	no change	Cl_2 not displaced	no reaction
I^-(aq)	brown solution and/or black precipitate	I_2 displaced	$2I^- + Br_2 \rightarrow 2Br^- + I_2$

Table 8
The reactions of $I_2(aq)$ with $Cl^-(aq)$ and $Br^-(aq)$

Halide	Observations	Conclusion	Equation
Cl^-(aq)	no change	Cl_2 not displaced	no reaction
Br^-(aq)	no change	Br_2 not displaced	no reaction

Essential Notes

Fluorine is far too dangerous to be used other than in specially equipped laboratories by specially-trained staff. However, experiments using fluorine have been carried out and show that fluorine will oxidise all other halide ions to the halogen.

These results confirm the order of oxidising power by showing that:

- chlorine will displace bromine and iodine
- bromine will displace iodine but not chlorine
- iodine will not displace either chlorine or bromine.

Trends in properties of the halides

Trends in the reducing ability of the halide ions

The ability of halogen molecules to behave as oxidising agents by accepting additional electrons to form halide ions was considered above. When a halide ion behaves as a reducing agent, it loses an electron to the reagent it is reducing; this process is the reverse of that in which a halogen molecule acts as an oxidising agent. The trend in reducing power of the halide ions shows a decrease from the strongly-reducing iodide ion to the non-reducing fluoride ion:

$$I^- > Br^- > Cl^- > F^-$$

Reactions of sodium halides with sulfuric acid

The trend in the reducing power of the halide ions is shown in the reaction of solid halide salts with concentrated sulfuric acid. The oxidation state of sulfur in sulfuric acid is $+6$. This can be reduced to $+4$, 0 or -2 depending on the reducing power of the halide ion. Experimental results are given in Table 9.

NaX	Observations	Products	Type of reaction
NaF	steamy fumes	HF	acid–base (F^- acting as a base)
NaCl	steamy fumes	HCl	acid–base (Cl^- acting as a base)
NaBr	steamy fumes	HBr	acid–base (Br^- acting as a base)
	colourless gas	SO_2	redox (reduction product of H_2SO_4)
	brown fumes	Br_2	redox (oxidation product of Br^-)
NaI	steamy fumes	HI	acid–base (I^- acting as a base)
	colourless gas	SO_2	redox (reduction product of H_2SO_4)
	yellow solid	S	redox (reduction product of H_2SO_4)
	smell of bad eggs	H_2S	redox (reduction product of H_2SO_4)
	black solid, purple fumes	I_2	redox (oxidation product of I^-)

Table 9
The reactions of concentrated sulfuric acid with solid sodium halides

Essential Notes

These reactions can be demonstrated in a laboratory fume cupboard but full safety precautions must be taken. Hydrogen fluoride is an extremely dangerous gas and, in the presence of water, will even etch glass.

These results indicate that:

- iodide ions can reduce the sulfur in H_2SO_4 from oxidation state +6 to +4, as SO_2, then to 0, as the element sulfur, and finally to −2, as H_2S
- bromide ions can reduce the sulfur in H_2SO_4 from oxidation state +6 to +4, as SO_2
- fluoride and chloride cannot reduce the sulfur in H_2SO_4 under these conditions.

Examiners' Notes

Deriving equations for the reactions which occur provides valuable revision of redox reactions.

Using aqueous solutions of silver nitrate and ammonia as a test for chloride, bromide and iodide ions in solution

Silver fluoride is soluble in water but silver chloride, silver bromide and silver iodide are all insoluble. Silver chloride, bromide and iodide are precipitated when an aqueous solution containing the appropriate halide ion is treated with an aqueous solution of silver nitrate. The colours of the three silver salts formed with chloride, bromide and iodide ions, and their different solubilities in aqueous ammonia, can be used as a test for the presence of the halide. These results are summarised in Table 10.

Essential Notes

Adding dilute nitric acid to the solution under test before the addition of silver nitrate solution prevents the formation of other insoluble compounds, such as Ag_2CO_3.

Halide	Precipitate	Observation	Solubility of precipitate in ammonia solution
F^-	none	–	–
Cl^-	AgCl	white solid	soluble in dilute $NH_3(aq)$
Br^-	AgBr	cream solid	sparingly soluble in dilute $NH_3(aq)$, soluble in concentrated $NH_3(aq)$
I^-	AgI	yellow solid	insoluble in concentrated $NH_3(aq)$

Table 10
Testing for halide ions using $AgNO_3(aq)$ and $NH_3(aq)$

Examiners' Notes

If you are asked to describe an observation, you must always link a colour to a solution or a solid (precipitate).

These results show that the solubility of the silver halides in ammonia solution decreases in the following order:

AgF > AgCl > AgBr > AgI

Uses of chlorine and chlorate(I)

The products obtained when chlorine reacts with water depend on the conditions used. Under normal laboratory conditions, a very pale green solution is formed, showing the presence of the element chlorine, and an equilibrium is established:

$$Cl_2 + H_2O \rightleftharpoons HCl + HClO$$

This reaction is an example of a **disproportionation** reaction in which one species, in this case chlorine, is simultaneously both oxidised and reduced:

Oxidation state of chlorine: 0 -1 $+1$

$$Cl_2 + H_2O \rightleftharpoons HCl + HClO$$

If universal indicator is added to a solution of chlorine water, it first turns red since both the reaction products are acids, i.e. hydrochloric acid, HCl, which is a strong (fully ionised) acid, and chloric(I) acid, HClO, which is a weak (slightly ionised) acid. The red colour then disappears and a colourless solution is left because chloric(I) acid is a very effective bleach.

If chlorine is bubbled through water in the presence of bright sunlight, or the green solution of chlorine water is left in bright sunlight, a colourless gas is produced and the green colour, due to chlorine, fades. Tests show that the colourless gas evolved is oxygen. Under these conditions, chlorine oxidises water to oxygen and is itself reduced to chloride ions:

$$2Cl_2 + 2H_2O \rightarrow 4H^+ + 4Cl^- + O_2$$

Water treatment

Chlorine and chlorine compounds are used in water treatment. For many years, small quantities of chlorine have been added to drinking water and to swimming pools in order to kill disease-causing bacteria. In drinking water, the major public health hazards are due to bacteria that cause cholera and typhus. In swimming pools, the dangerous bacteria killed by chlorine are often types of *E. coli* that originate from human waste.

The concentration of chlorine in drinking water is approximately 0.7 mg dm^{-3}. Higher concentrations are used in swimming pools. Great care is taken to ensure that the correct amounts of chlorine are used because chlorine itself is very toxic. In addition, chlorine can react with organic waste material in water to form organochlorine compounds which may be toxic. Although it is well known that failure to chlorinate water results in serious health risks, there is little information to support the claim that the formation of organochlorine compounds in water is a long-term health risk.

Reaction of chlorine with cold dilute aqueous sodium hydroxide

When chlorine reacts with cold water, an equilibrium is established between the reactants and the two acidic products:

$$Cl_2 + H_2O \rightleftharpoons HCl + HClO$$

Essential Notes

Because this reaction is rather slow, it is best to leave an inverted test tube containing chlorine water in sunlight for several days, after which sufficient oxygen will have been produced to give a positive test with a glowing splint.

If water is replaced by cold dilute sodium hydroxide, the effect is to displace the equilibrium to the right as the hydroxide ions react with the acids produced:

$$Cl_2 + 2NaOH \rightarrow NaCl + NaClO + H_2O$$

$$\text{or } Cl_2 + 2OH^- \rightarrow Cl^- + ClO^- + H_2O$$

This reaction is of great commercial importance because the mixture of sodium chloride and sodium chlorate(I) is used as a bleach.

3.2.6 Group 2, the alkaline earth metals

The Group 2 elements are the metals in the second group of the Periodic Table. They are therefore s-block elements in which the outermost electrons are in a full s sub-shell.

Trends in physical properties

Some important physical properties of the Group 2 elements Mg–Ba are given in Table 11.

Element	Electron configuration	Atomic radius/nm	First ionisation energy/kJ mol^{-1}	Melting point/K
Mg	[Ne]3s^2	0.136	737	924
Ca	[Ar]4s^2	0.174	590	1116
Sr	[Kr]5s^2	0.191	549	1042
Ba	[Xe]6s^2	0.198	503	998

Table 11
Physical properties of the Group 2 elements Mg–Ba

Essential Notes

Remember, electron configurations are sometimes abbreviated by giving only the electrons beyond the previous noble gas.

Atomic radius
On descending the group from magnesium to barium, the atomic radii increase. This trend is due to the increasing number of electron shells, resulting in the outermost electrons being progressively further away from the nucleus (see Fig 14).

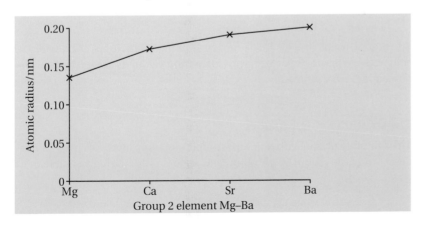

Fig 14
Atomic radius of the Group 2 elements Mg–Ba

First ionisation energy

The first ionisation energies of the elements decrease down the group as the atomic radius increases and the outermost electrons become increasingly shielded from the positive charge of the nucleus.

Melting points

The Group 2 elements are metals with high melting points (see Fig 15). In metallic structures, the positive ions, (cations) (M^{2+} in this group) are surrounded by a 'sea' of outermost electrons. There are two of these delocalised electrons for each M^{2+} ion. As the metal ions become larger going down the group, the strength of the metallic bonds generally decreases, because the decreasing density of charge (or charge-to-size ratio) of the ions means that there is less attraction for the delocalised electrons. The expected general decrease in melting point from calcium to strontium can be seen. Magnesium has a lower melting point than expected because it has a different crystal structure from the other metals.

Essential Notes

Magnesium has a hexagonal close-packed structure, calcium and strontium have face-centred cubic structures and barium has a body-centred cubic structure.

Fig 15
Melting points of the
Group 2 elements Mg–Ba

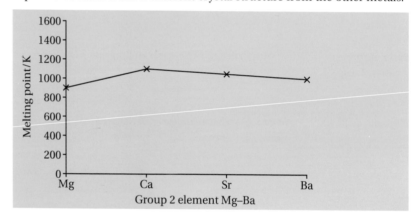

Trends in chemical properties

Reactions with water

The reactivity of the Group 2 elements with water increases on descending the group. Magnesium reacts only very slowly with cold water:

$$Mg(s) + H_2O(l) \rightarrow Mg(OH)_2(s) + H_2(g)$$

Burning magnesium reacts rapidly with steam:

$$Mg(s) + H_2O(g) \rightarrow MgO(s) + H_2(g)$$

The other Group 2 metals – calcium, strontium and barium – react with cold water, releasing hydrogen with increasing vigour as the group is descended. For example:

$$Ca(s) + 2H_2O(l) \rightarrow Ca(OH)_2(aq) + H_2(g)$$

The solubility of hydroxides

The solubility of the hydroxides of Group 2 elements increases on descending the group. Magnesium hydroxide is only sparingly soluble in water. Calcium hydroxide dissolves to form 'lime water', but is not as soluble as strontium hydroxide, while barium hydroxide is soluble in water and produces strongly alkaline solutions:

$$Ba(OH)_2(s) + aq \rightarrow Ba^{2+}(aq) + 2OH^-(aq)$$

Uses of magnesium and calcium hydroxides

Magnesium hydroxide is used as an antacid for the relief of indigestion caused by an excess of acid in the stomach:

$$Mg(OH)_2(s) + 2H^+(aq) \rightarrow Mg^{2+}(aq) + 2H_2O(l)$$

Magnesium hydroxide also acts as a laxative and is used to relieve constipation. It is taken orally either as chewable tablets or in a suspension often called 'milk of magnesia'.

Calcium hydroxide is used by farmers to reduce soil acidity, so that a wider range of crops can be grown, and to provide calcium ions which are essential for plant growth. The 'lime' used by farmers is often a mixture of calcium carbonate together with calcium hydroxide.

The solubility of sulfates

The solubility of the sulfates of Group 2 elements decreases from the soluble magnesium sulfate to the insoluble barium sulfate.

In the laboratory, the insolubility of barium sulfate is used as a test for the presence of sulfate ions in solution. Dilute acid (hydrochloric or nitric) and a solution of barium ions (from barium chloride or barium nitrate) are added to the solution under test and the appearance of a white precipitate indicates the presence of sulfate ions:

$$Ba^{2+}(aq) + SO_4^{2-}(aq) \rightarrow BaSO_4(s)$$

In the absence of acids, carbonate ions interfere with this test because barium carbonate is also a white solid, insoluble in water. The carbonate ions are removed by adding either hydrochloric or nitric acid. The acid reacts with the carbonate ions to generate carbon dioxide gas, thereby removing them from solution and preventing the precipitation of barium carbonate:

$$2H^+(aq) + CO_3^{2-}(aq) \rightarrow CO_2(g) + H_2O(l)$$

Use of barium sulfate in medicine

Because barium sulfate blocks X-rays and is not toxic (as it is so insoluble in water or body fluids), it is used in medicine to aid the investigation of problems in digestive and bowel systems. An aqueous suspension of barium sulfate is taken orally, if an image of the digestive system is required, or injected through the anus, if images of the bowel region are needed.

3.2.7 Extraction of metals

The production of metals is an important part of the chemical manufacturing industry. The way in which metals are produced from natural sources involves an understanding of the social and economic aspects of the processes, as well as an appreciation of the underlying chemistry.

One of the jobs of a chemist is to transform the lumps of rock all around us into useful materials. Metals are important materials – they are used for their strength, their ductility, and their thermal and electrical conductivities.

Oxide and sulfide ores

Metals usually occur naturally in combination with oxygen or sulfur. The process of extraction is therefore one of reduction – often of oxides. Because oxide ores are very stable compounds, energy usually must be put in to reduce them to metal; i.e. extraction reactions are endothermic (unless a very powerful reducing agent such as aluminium metal is used).

Sulfide ores are not usually reduced directly to the metals. They are first roasted in air to produce oxides; this process liberates sulfur dioxide and so potentially gives rise to the pollution hazard of acid rain. Sulfur dioxide dissolves in water in the clouds to form sulfurous acid according to the equation:

$$SO_2(g) + H_2O(l) \rightarrow H_2SO_3(aq)$$

Some of the sulfur dioxide is oxidised to sulfur trioxide:

$$2SO_2(g) + O_2(g) \rightarrow 2SO_3(g)$$

This gas dissolves in water to form sulfuric acid:

$$SO_3(g) + H_2O(l) \rightarrow H_2SO_4(aq)$$

These acids can then fall as acid rain, damaging plants and polluting lakes.

The sulfur dioxide produced by the roasting of sulfide ores is collected, purified and used to manufacture sulfuric acid. Electrostatic precipitators are used to remove dust, after which the gas is washed with water and finally dried with concentrated sulfuric acid before being used in the **contact process**.

Extraction

There are many ways by which metal oxides can be reduced to metals. The method actually chosen on an industrial scale for each metal depends upon several factors, including:

- the cost of the reducing agent
- the cost of energy for the process
- the required purity of the metal.

Reduction of metal oxides with carbon

Carbon is a cheap and plentiful reducing agent – it occurs in coal (which when heated in the absence of air gives coke, a solid with a very high carbon content) and in charcoal (which is obtained from wood, a renewable resource). All metal oxides can, in theory, be reduced by carbon if the temperature is high enough. In practice, temperatures over 2000 °C are impractical and uneconomic.

Iron, manganese and copper

Iron oxides are reduced by coke in a blast furnace. Initially, coke reacts with a hot air blast in a strongly exothermic reaction:

$$C(s) + O_2(g) \rightarrow 2CO_2(g)$$

This reaction produces the heat needed for the reduction of the iron(III) oxide. The carbon dioxide formed reacts at high temperature with unreacted coke to form carbon monoxide:

$$CO_2(g) + C(s) \rightarrow 2CO(g)$$

The carbon monoxide reduces most of the iron(III) oxide at around 1200 °C:

$$Fe_2O_3(s) + 3CO(g) \rightarrow 2Fe(l) + 3CO_2(g)$$

In the hotter part of the furnace, coke also reacts directly with the iron oxide:

$$Fe_2O_3(s) + 3C(s) \rightarrow 2Fe(l) + 3CO(g)$$

Impure manganese is produced when manganese(IV) oxide is heated with carbon:

$$MnO_2(s) + C(s) \rightarrow Mn(l) + CO_2(g)$$

This method is used to make ferromanganese. This alloy of iron and manganese is produced by the thermal reduction of a mixture of iron and manganese oxides with carbon.

Copper is formed when copper(II) oxide is heated with carbon, but this process is only suitable when starting from ores which contain a high percentage of copper:

$$2CuO(s) + C(s) \rightarrow 2Cu(l) + CO_2(g)$$

The copper obtained by carbon reduction is impure and, for most purposes, needs to be purified.

Carbide formation

Some metals form metal carbides rather than the metal itself when the oxide is heated with carbon. Reduction by carbon is not a practical method of extracting these metals. Examples include the oxides of titanium, tungsten and aluminium.

Reduction of aluminium oxide by electrolysis

When the metal oxide is extremely stable, then electrolytic methods may be used. The manufacture of aluminium is carried out by the electrolysis of purified bauxite, Al_2O_3, which is dissolved in molten cryolite, Na_3AlF_6. The melting point of aluminium oxide is over 2000 °C, but by dissolving the oxide in molten cryolite, the temperature of the melt is reduced to about 970 °C. The electrodes are made of carbon and the reactions at the electrodes are:

at the cathode: $Al^{3+}(l) + 3e^- \rightarrow Al(l)$

at the anode: $2O^{2-}(l) \rightarrow O_2(g) + 4e^-$

Some of the oxygen evolved reacts with the carbon anodes at the high temperature:

$2C(s) + O_2(g) \rightarrow 2CO(g)$

and

$C(s) + O_2(g) \rightarrow CO_2(g)$

The process consumes large amounts of electricity (because electricity is needed to melt the cryolite and to decompose the Al_2O_3) and is economic only where electricity is relatively inexpensive. The process is continuous, but regular additions of aluminium oxide are needed, and the carbon anodes need replacing as they are consumed. There is a potential environmental problem through waste cryolite causing fluoride pollution.

Extraction of titanium

Titanium is obtained from its oxide in two steps.

Step 1: Conversion of titanium(IV) oxide into titanium(IV) chloride

The ore rutile, impure titanium(IV) oxide, is converted into titanium(IV) chloride using chlorine and coke at around 900 °C:

$TiO_2(s) + 2C(s) + 2Cl_2(g) \rightarrow TiCl_4(g) + 2CO(g)$

At room temperature, titanium(IV) chloride is a colourless liquid which fumes in moist air because of hydrolysis. It is purified from other chlorides (e.g. those of iron, silicon and chromium) by fractional distillation under argon or nitrogen.

Step 2: Reduction of titanium(IV) chloride by a reactive metal

In the United Kingdom, titanium(IV) chloride is reduced by sodium in the following exothermic reaction:

$TiCl_4(l) + 4Na(l) \rightarrow Ti(s) + 4NaCl(s)$

The sodium is initially held at around 550 °C, but the temperature rises to nearly 1000 °C during the reaction. An inert atmosphere of argon is used to prevent any contamination of the metal with oxygen or nitrogen. The sodium chloride by-product is washed out, leaving titanium as a granular powder.

Elsewhere in the world, magnesium is used as the reducing agent in a similar reduction process:

$$TiCl_4(l) + 2Mg(l) \rightarrow Ti(s) + 2MgCl_2(s)$$

The magnesium chloride by-product is removed from the titanium by vacuum distillation at high temperature.

Reduction of tungsten(VI) oxide by hydrogen

Tungsten is produced when tungsten(VI) oxide is heated to a high temperature in hydrogen:

$$WO_3(s) + 3H_2(g) \rightarrow W(s) + 3H_2O(g)$$

This method produces pure tungsten as a powder. There is, however, always a fire or explosion risk when working with hydrogen, especially at high temperatures.

Environmental aspects of metal extraction

The recycling of metals is carried out extensively. It would be environmentally friendly if all scrap were returned to the metal works and recycled. Unfortunately, because scrap metal is widely spread and often many miles from metal-producing plants, the scrap must first be collected and transported. This procedure creates an energy cost which must be calculated carefully and offset against the savings made in extraction.

Scrap metal contains a higher percentage of metal than a commercial ore and, without recycling, serious environmental problems would result from discarded scrap.

The extraction methods for many metals produce carbon dioxide, a 'greenhouse gas'; re-melting does not produce large amounts of this gas although some may be evolved in producing the energy required for the recycling process.

Extraction of copper from dilute aqueous solutions of its ions

Copper can be extracted from an aqueous solution by the addition of a more reactive metal. Scrap iron, which is readily available and cheap, is often used:

$$Cu^{2+}(aq) + Fe(s) \rightarrow Cu(s) + Fe^{2+}(aq)$$

This process is used when copper is extracted from copper-containing waste or from low-grade ore (ore containing a low percentage of copper). An aqueous solution containing copper(II) ions is obtained when the waste, or low-grade ore, is treated either with dilute sulfuric acid or with an aqueous solution of an enzyme which catalyses the formation of copper(II) ions.

No heat energy is required for this extraction process, no carbon dioxide is evolved and more effective use is made of the Earth's resources.

3.2.8 Haloalkanes

The haloalkanes are the homologous series of compounds with the general formula $C_nH_{2n+1}X$ where X is a halogen, i.e. F, Cl, Br or I, for example:

- CH_3CH_2Cl chloroethane
- $CH_3CHBrCH_3$ 2-bromopropane.

Synthesis of chloroalkanes

Alkanes such as methane do not react with chlorine at room temperature or in the dark. In the presence of ultra-violet light, however, a mixture of methane and chlorine will react at room temperature, forming hydrogen chloride and a mixture of chlorinated methanes. The mechanism for this process is called **free-radical substitution**.

A free radical (or radical for short) is a species which contains an odd number of electrons with one electron not paired with any other. Radicals can be single atoms or groups of atoms. A radical is represented by writing a dot (as in Cl•) to indicate the unpaired electron. Radicals are formed when a covalent bond breaks with an equal splitting of the bonding pair of electrons (homolytic fission).

The free-radical substitution **mechanism** occurs in several steps.

Initiation step

$$Cl_2 \rightarrow 2Cl•$$

The ultra-violet light provides the energy needed to start the reaction by splitting some chlorine molecules into atoms (radicals). This process occurs first because the Cl—Cl bond in chlorine is weaker than the C—H bond in methane.

Propagation steps

$$Cl• + CH_4 \rightarrow •CH_3 + HCl$$

$$•CH_3 + Cl_2 \rightarrow CH_3Cl + Cl•$$

In each step, a radical is used and a new radical is formed, so that the process continues and leads to a **chain reaction**. Each step is exothermic, so that the chain reaction might produce an explosion. The overall reaction, which is the sum of the two propagation steps, can be represented by the equation:

$$CH_4 + Cl_2 \rightarrow CH_3Cl + HCl$$

Termination steps

When two radicals combine, they form a stable molecule and the sequence of reactions stops; the unpaired electrons in the radicals pair up to form a covalent bond. Two possible termination steps are:

$$Cl• + •CH_3 \rightarrow CH_3Cl$$

$$•CH_3 + •CH_3 \rightarrow CH_3CH_3$$

Such termination steps can lead to trace amounts of impurities, such as ethane, in the final product.

Examiners' Notes

Ultra-violet light consists of very high-energy radiation, enough to break the Cl—Cl bond

Essential Notes

A **mechanism** is a method used by organic chemists to show how a reaction occurs; i.e. what happens to the electrons as the bonds in the reactants break and new bonds are formed in the products.

Examiners' Notes

Chlorination of propane produces two monochloropropanes, 1-chloropropane and 2-chloropropane, in an approximate ratio of 3:1 because of the ratio of 6 CH_3 hydrogens to 2 CH_2 hydrogens in propane.

The termination step:

$$Cl\bullet + Cl\bullet \rightarrow Cl_2$$

is possible, but unlikely because the chlorine radicals collide with enough energy to separate again immediately.

Further substitution

The reaction of a chlorine radical with methane extracts a hydrogen radical (atom) to form HCl, as shown in the first propagation step. Chloromethane still contains three hydrogen atoms, and so further pairs of propagation steps are possible, leading to dichloromethane (CH_2Cl_2), trichloromethane ($CHCl_3$) and finally to tetrachloromethane (CCl_4). The propagation steps to form CH_2Cl_2 are:

$$Cl\bullet + CH_3Cl \rightarrow \bullet CH_2Cl + HCl$$

$$\bullet CH_2Cl + Cl_2 \rightarrow CH_2Cl_2 + Cl\bullet$$

The likelihood of further substitution beyond the formation of CH_3Cl can be reduced if an excess of methane is used.

Similar free-radical substitution reactions can also occur with fluorine and bromine.

Uses of chloroalkanes and chlorofluoroalkanes

Haloalkanes have been used for many purposes, such as anaesthetics, refrigerants, aerosol propellants, insecticides and solvents. Their use for these purposes has become controversial as evidence has been discovered of the toxicity of some haloalkanes and also of the effects of others on the atmosphere.

Toxicity of haloalkanes

The chloroalkane 1,1,1-trichloroethane, CH_3CCl_3, was formerly used as a dry-cleaning solvent to remove grease on clothes and also as the thinner for correcting fluids. Tetrachloromethane (carbon tetrachloride), CCl_4, was also used by dry cleaners as a solvent. Both of these compounds are now classed as toxic (poisonous) and their use is no longer allowed.

Effects of CFCs on the ozone layer

Hydrocarbons in which all the hydrogen atoms have been substituted by both chlorine and fluorine atoms are called chlorofluorocarbons or CFCs (see Fig 16).

Because of the strength of the C—F and C—Cl bonds (see page 43), these compounds are very unreactive. Their volatility and inertness made them attractive for use as refrigerants, as aerosol propellants and in packaging materials such as expanded polystyrene. However, although this unreactive nature was beneficial in these uses, it was discovered that CFCs were a threat to the ozone layer in the upper atmosphere, and so they are no longer used.

Ozone, or trioxygen, O_3, is an allotrope of oxygen. It is formed when ultraviolet radiation from the sun breaks down oxygen molecules, O_2, into two oxygen atoms (radicals). These oxygen radicals then react with more oxygen to form ozone.

Fig 16
Examples of CFCs

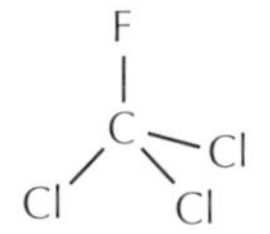

trichlorofluoromethane, CCl_3F, known as CFC-11

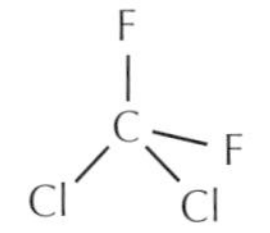

dichlorodifluoromethane, CCl_2F_2, known as CFC-12

Fig 17
Formation and decomposition of Ozone

$$O_2 \xrightarrow{UV} 2O\bullet$$

$$O\bullet + O_2 \rightarrow \bullet O_3$$

$$\bullet O_3 \xrightarrow{UV} O_2 + O\bullet$$

$$O\bullet + \bullet O_3 \rightarrow 2O_2$$

Strictly, oxygen should be shown as $\bullet O\bullet$ because it has two separate unpaired electrons.

Ultra-violet radiation also decomposes ozone into an oxygen molecule and an oxygen radical, which can react with more ozone to reform O_2 molecules (Fig 17).

The overall result of these reactions is that the presence of ozone in the upper atmosphere reduces the amount of harmful ultra-violet radiation from the sun that can reach the Earth's surface.

However, in the 1970s, it was discovered that the ozone 'layer' over Antarctica was considerably thinner than expected and the reason for this was found to be the reaction of chlorine radicals with ozone. These chlorine radicals are formed in the upper atmosphere when ultra-violet radiation causes the C—Cl bond in CFCs to break, for example:

$$CF_2Cl_2 \rightarrow Cl\bullet + \bullet CF_2Cl$$

The following is a possible sequence of reactions that then occur:

$$Cl\bullet + O_3 \rightarrow ClO\bullet + O_2$$

$$ClO\bullet + O_3 \rightarrow Cl\bullet + 2O_2$$

Fig 18
Examples of HFCs

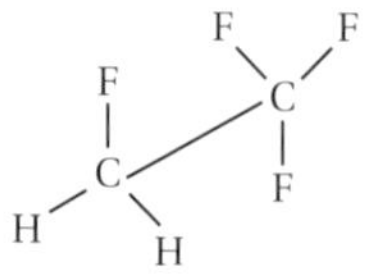

HFC 134a

HFC 152a

Chlorine radicals are removed in the first reaction but are re-formed in the second; overall, they are not used up and so are acting as a catalyst for the decomposition of ozone. This situation means that even small amounts of chlorine radicals can continue to deplete the ozone layer for many years.

As a result of this evidence, the use of CFCs was banned by international agreement (the Montreal protocol) and chemists have developed suitable replacements which do not contain chlorine. The most common of these are HFCs, which contain hydrogen, fluorine and carbon, such as CH_2FCF_3 (known as HFC 134a) and CH_3CHF_2 (known as HFC 152a) (see Fig 18). Since C—F bonds are stronger than C—Cl they are less likely to be broken by ultra-violet radiation. However, chemists will continue to monitor the atmosphere to check that these replacements do not themselves cause any long-term problems.

Nucleophilic substitution

Halogen atoms are electronegative (see Table 12) so that carbon–halogen bonds in haloalkanes are polar. The electrons in the C—X bond are attracted towards the halogen atom, which gains a slight negative charge, $\delta-$, leaving the carbon atom electron-deficient or with a slight positive charge, $\delta+$.

The $\delta+$ carbon is then susceptible to attack by nucleophiles; i.e. negative ions or molecules with a lone pair of electrons. When nucleophilic attack occurs, the carbon–halogen bond breaks and a halide ion is released. The nucleophile replaces the halogen atom in a substitution reaction. The mechanism of this reaction (shown in Fig 19) is called **nucleophilic substitution**.

Table 12
Electronegativity values

Element	Electronegativity
C	2.5
F	4.0
Cl	3.0
Br	2.8
I	2.5

Fig 19
Nucleophilic substitution

$$\ddot{Nu} \quad \overset{\delta+}{CH_3} \overset{\delta-}{-Br} \longrightarrow \overset{+}{Nu}-CH_3 + :Br^-$$

The rate of such reactions is influenced by the strength of the carbon–halogen bond (see Table 13). Although the C—F bond is very polar, fluoroalkanes are very unreactive because the bond is so strong;

Essential Notes

$\ddot{Nu}$ represents any nucleophile, an electron-pair donor.

chloroalkanes are also fairly slow to react. Carbon–bromine bonds, however, are more easily broken so that bromoalkanes react at a reasonable rate.

Bond	C—F	C—Cl	C—Br	C—I
Mean bond enthalpy/ kJ mol^{-1}	484	338	276	238

Table 13
Carbon–halogen bond strengths (mean bond enthalpies)

Nucleophilic substitution reactions

Nucleophilic substitution with hydroxide ions

When haloalkanes are warmed with aqueous sodium hydroxide or potassium hydroxide, alcohols are formed (see Fig 20).

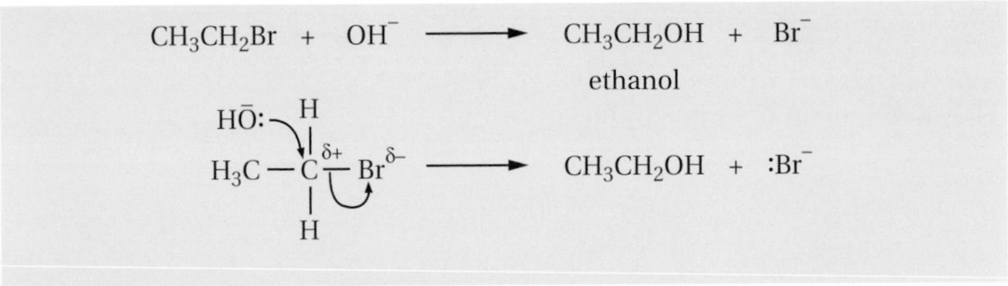

Essential Notes

This process is sometimes called *hydrolysis*.

Fig 20
Equation and mechanism for the formation of ethanol

Nucleophilic substitution with cyanide ions

When haloalkanes are warmed with an aqueous/alcoholic solution of potassium cyanide, nitriles are formed. For example, see Fig 21.

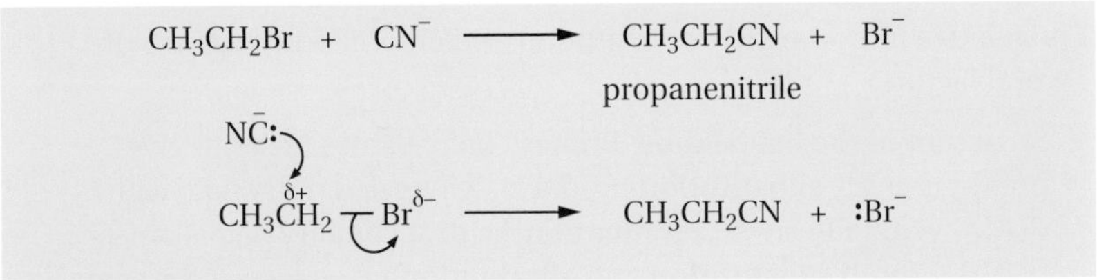

Essential Notes

Nucleophilic substitution with cyanide ions adds an extra carbon to the chain. Compounds of the homologous series RCN are called nitriles.

Fig 21
Equation and mechanism for the formation of propanenitrile

Nucleophilic substitution with ammonia

When haloalkanes are warmed with an excess of ammonia in a sealed container, primary amines are formed. For example, bromoethane forms ethylamine:

$$CH_3CH_2Br + NH_3 \rightarrow CH_3CH_2NH_2 + HBr$$
$$\text{ethylamine}$$

Since the acid HBr immediately reacts with the base NH_3, this equation is more correctly written as:

$$CH_3CH_2Br + 2NH_3 \rightarrow CH_3CH_2NH_2 + NH_4Br$$

The mechanism has two steps, as shown in Fig 22.

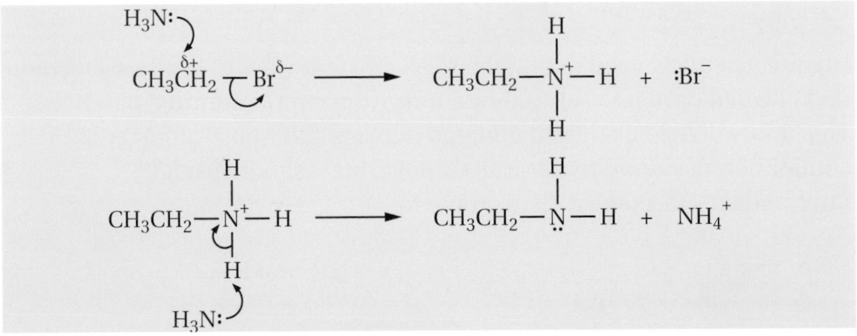

Essential Notes

Reduction of a nitrile using hydrogen in the presence of a nickel catalyst also forms a primary amine (see *Collins Student Support Materials: Unit 4 – Kinetics, Equilibria and Organic Chemistry*, section 3.4.7).

Examiners' Notes

Primary amines contain the NH_2 functional group.

Fig 22
Mechanism for the formation of ethylamine

The excess of ammonia minimises the chance of further reaction of the primary amines to form secondary or tertiary amines, or quaternary ammonium salts (see *Collins Students Support Materials: Unit 4 – Kinetics, Equilibria and Organic Chemistry*, section 3.4.7).

Elimination

In the reaction between aqueous sodium hydroxide and a haloalkane, the hydroxide ion acts as a nucleophile, and an alcohol is formed by nucleophilic substitution. However, the hydroxide ion can also function as a base, so an alternative **elimination** reaction also takes place in which hydrogen and a halogen are eliminated from the haloalkane and an alkene is formed. For example:

$$CH_3CHBrCH_3 + OH^- \rightarrow CH_3CH = CH_2 + H_2O + Br^-$$

2-bromopropane   propene

The mechanism is shown in Fig 23.

Fig 23
Formation of propene by an
elimination reaction

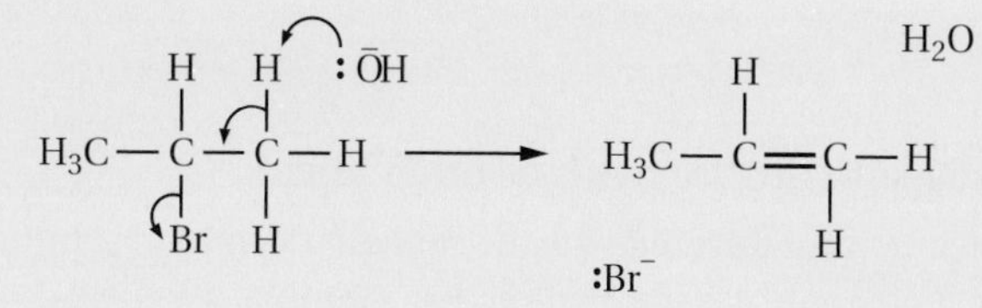

The relative importance of substitution and elimination depends on several factors:

- **Structure of the haloalkane**: Primary haloalkanes (RCH_2X) give predominantly **substitution** products, whereas tertiary haloakanes (R_3CX) generally favour **elimination**. With secondary haloalkanes (R_2CHX), both **substitution** and **elimination** take place at the same time (concurrently).

- **Base strength of the nucleophile**: The likelihood of elimination increases as the base strength of the nucleophile increases.

- **Reaction conditions**: Higher reaction temperatures lead to a greater proportion of elimination.

In the reaction of 2-bromopropane with potassium hydroxide (see above), both substitution and elimination reactions occur together:

- elimination is favoured by hot ethanolic conditions
- substitution is favoured by warm aqueous conditions.

Organic synthesis

Organic chemists need to find the most efficient ways of synthesising more complicated or more useful compounds from simple starting materials. The ability of haloalkanes to undergo nucleophilic substitution and elimination reactions, as described above, makes them useful intermediates in such synthetic routes.

Examiners' Notes

Depending on the structure of the haloalkane, more than one alkene may be formed. Thus, for example, elimination from 2-bromobutane produces both but-1-ene and but-2-ene. The latter compound can, of course, exist as two E–Z stereoisomers; E-but-2-ene and Z-but-2-ene (see section 3.2.7).

Essential Notes

Aqueous NaOH contains the nucleophile HO^- and NaOH in ethanol also contains the stronger base $CH_3CH_2O^-$.

3.2.9 Alkenes

Alkenes: structure, bonding and reactivity

The alkenes are a homologous series of hydrocarbons with the general formula C_nH_{2n}. The first three members are:

- ethene $\qquad$ C_2H_4
- propene $\qquad$ C_3H_6
- butene $\qquad$ C_4H_8

Alkenes contain two hydrogen atoms fewer than their parent alkanes and are said to be **unsaturated**. This term is used because alkenes contain a double covalent bond between two carbon atoms (see Fig 24) and so they can become saturated by the addition of hydrogen.

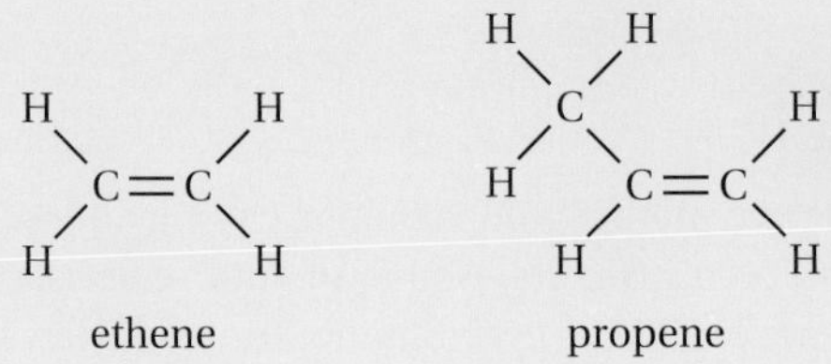

Examiners' Notes

The general formula for alkenes, C_nH_{2n}, can also represent cyclic alkanes. For example, C_6H_{12} can represent several isomeric hexenes and also cycloalkanes such as cyclohexane, methylcyclopentane and dimethylcyclobutane.

ethene $\qquad\qquad$ propene

Fig 24
Structures of ethene and propene

E–Z stereoisomerism

Carbon–carbon double bonds in alkenes cannot easily rotate because of the electron clouds present above and below the plane of the bond. When an alkene has two different groups at each end of the double bond, two different *E–Z* stereoisomers result. These compounds have the same structural formula, but the bonds within the molecule are arranged differently in space.

Essential Notes

E stands for entgegen (German for opposite). *Z* stands for zusammen (German for together). *E–Z* stereoisomerism is also known as *geometrical* or *cis–trans* isomerism.

Definition

Stereoisomers are compounds which have the same structural formula but the bonds are arranged differently in space.

There are two types of stereoisomerism, *E–Z* **stereoisomerism**, discussed here, and **optical isomerism** which is discussed in *Collins Student Support Materials: Unit 4 – Kinetics, Equilibria and Organic Chemistry*, section 3.4.4.

E means that two groups, which may be identical, are on opposite sides of the double bond and *Z* means they are on the same side. For example, but-2-ene exists as two forms that differ only in the arrangement of the bonds in space (see Fig 25).

Examiners' Notes

The double bond results from the overlap of two spare, unbonded, singly filled p orbitals, one present on each carbon atom in the bond:

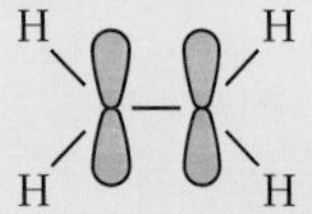

This overlap produces an electron cloud above and below the molecule (a π bond):

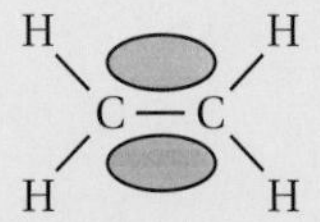

The two carbon atoms of the double bond and the four atoms attached to the double bond must lie in the same plane:

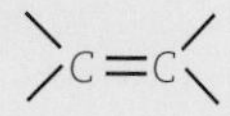

Therefore ethene is a planar molecule.

Fig 25
The two *E–Z* stereoisomers of but-2-ene

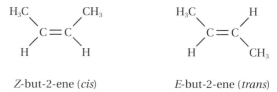

Z-but-2-ene (*cis*)　　　　E-but-2-ene (*trans*)

Examiners' Notes

E–Z isomers are possible because rotation at a double bond requires a significant input of energy (too much energy to be supplied at room temperature); this situation is referred to as restricted rotation.

Note that methylpropene is a structural isomer, but not an *E–Z* stereoisomer of but-2-ene, because it is not possible to have *E–Z* stereoisomerism when there are two identical groups joined to the same carbon atom in a double bond (see Fig 26).

Fig 26
Structure of methylpropene

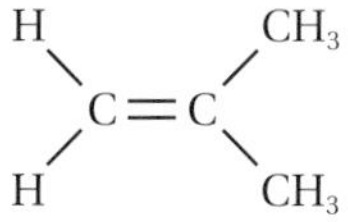

methylpropene

Methylpropene has two methyl groups on one carbon and two hydrogen atoms on the other. It is a structural isomer of but-2-ene, as also are but-1-ene and the cyclic alkanes cyclobutane and methylcyclopropane. (see Fig 27)

Fig 27
The structure of methylpropene

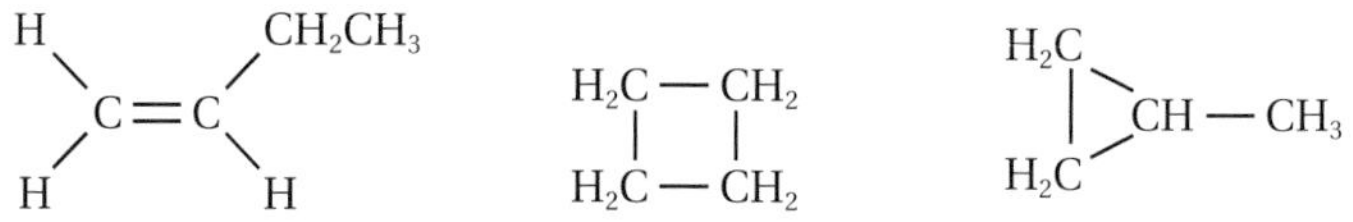

but-1-ene　　　　cyclobutane　　　　methylcyclopropane

Examiners' Notes

E–Z stereoisomers have different physical and chemical properties. Z-isomers usually have slightly higher boiling points as they will have some polarity, whereas E-isomers are less polar. The boiling point of Z-but-2-ene is 4 °C whereas the boiling point of E-but-2-ene is 1 °C. E-isomers, however, often have higher melting points because they pack together better. For example, the melting point of Z-but-2-ene is −139 °C whereas the melting point of E-but-2-ene is −106 °C.

Electrophilic addition reactions of alkenes

The double bond in alkenes is an area of high electron density and is the cause of their reactivity. Alkenes can become saturated by the addition of small molecules across the double bond. In these reactions the C=C double bond becomes a C—C single bond.

The reaction of alkenes with small molecules such as HBr, H_2SO_4 or Br_2 occurs by an **electrophilic addition** mechanism:

- *electrophilic* because the electron-rich double bond attracts positive ions or electron-deficient atoms, and such species are called *electrophiles*
- *addition* because the electrophile joins on to the alkene to form one new molecule.

Hydrogen bromide

Alkenes react with hydrogen bromide in the gas phase, or in concentrated aqueous solution, to form bromoalkanes. For example ethene reacts to form bromoethane (see Fig 2.8).

Examiners' Notes

Electrophiles are positive ions or electron-deficient atoms and act as electron-pair acceptors; they seek electron-rich sites.

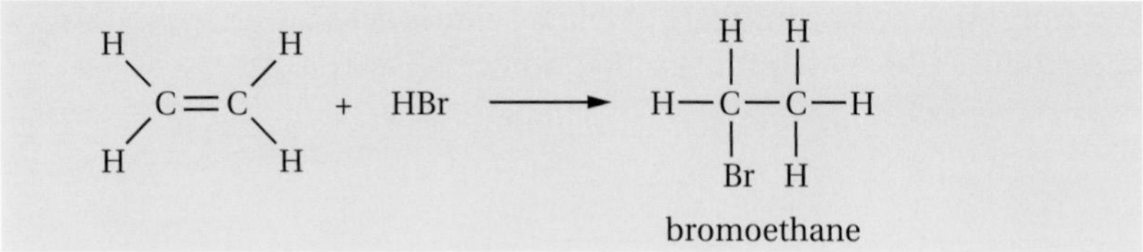

Fig 28
Equation for the reaction of ethene with HBr

The overall process involves electrophilic addition across a C=C double bond. The mechanism in the gas phase is shown in Fig 29.

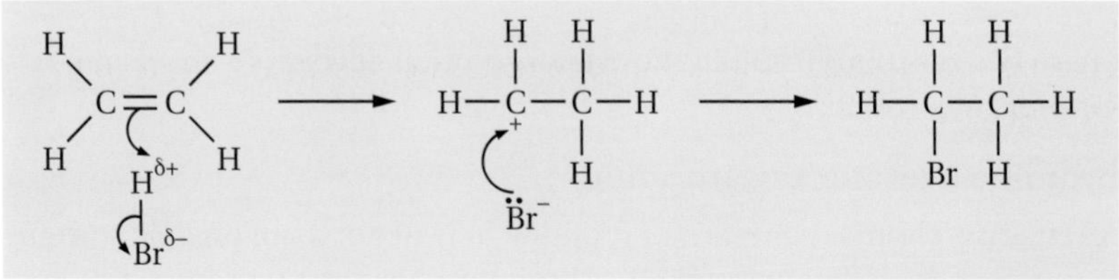

Fig 29
Elecrophilic addition mechanism for the reaction of ethene with HBr in the gas phase.

The curly arrows in Fig 29 each represent the movement of a *pair* of electrons. Arrows start either at a lone pair or at the middle of a bond. Arrows end either between the atoms, where the new covalent bond forms, or as a lone pair on an atom.

- Bromine is more electronegative than hydrogen, so the HBr molecule is polar. The electron-deficient or δ+ hydrogen atom acts as the electrophile (*electron-seeking species*).

- As electrons from the double bond move to form a new carbon-to-hydrogen bond with the δ+ hydrogen, the electrons in the hydrogen–bromine bond shift towards the bromine atom and the H—Br bond breaks, releasing a bromide ion. The other carbon in the double bond becomes an electron-deficient **carbocation**.

- The bromide ion then acts as a nucleophile; it uses a lone pair of electrons to form a new bond with the positive carbon in the carbocation.

When the reaction is performed in aqueous solution, $H^+(aq)$ ions act as electrophiles in the first step of the mechanism. In the second step, bromide ions attack the carbocation, as in the mechanism shown in Fig 29.

Sulfuric acid

Alkenes are absorbed by cold, concentrated sulfuric acid to form alkyl hydrogensulfates. For example, Fig 30 shows how ethene forms ethyl hydrogensulfate.

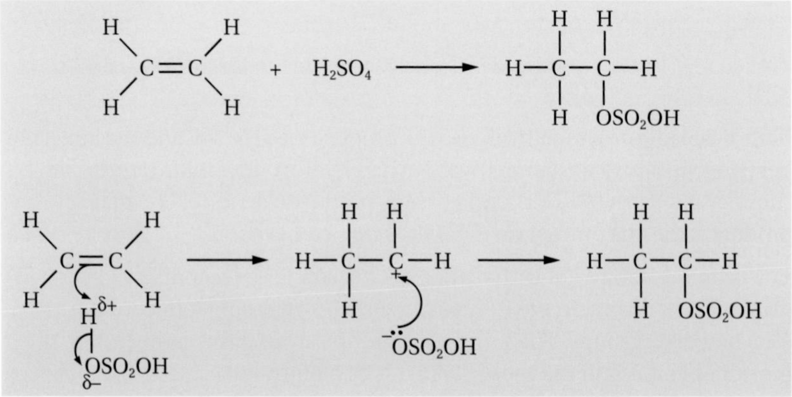

Essential Notes

A **carbocation** is a species which contains a carbon atom that has a positive charge.

Fig 30
Equation and mechanism for the reaction of ethene with concentrated sulfuric acid

Examiners' Notes

Ethanol is produced industrially by the direct hydration of ethene (see page 49) or by fermentation (see section 3.2.10).

Warming ethyl hydrogensulfate in dilute sulfuric acid causes hydrolysis and produces ethanol by the reaction shown in Fig 31.

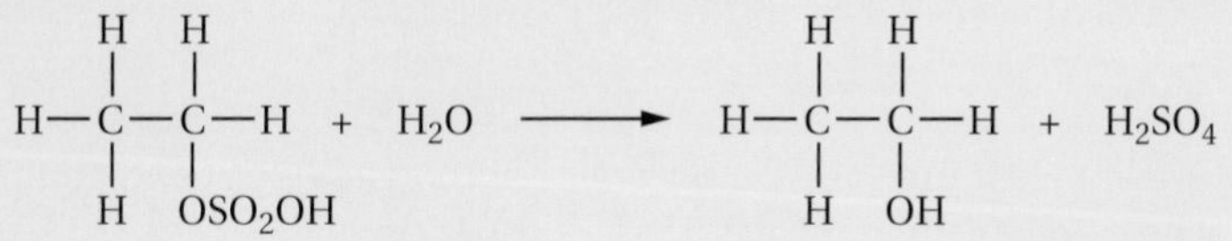

Fig 31
Hydrolysis of ethyl hydrogensulfate

Essential Notes

The amount of unsaturation in a margarine can be found by dissolving a sample in hexane and adding drops of bromine (*toxic and corrosive*). The more drops of bromine that are decolourised, the more unsaturation is present.

These two reactions result in the overall addition of water to an alkene, forming an alcohol.

Bromine a test for unsaturation

Alkenes decolourise solutions of bromine in water or in an organic solvent. Removal of the red–brown colour of bromine shows the presence of unsaturation, typically a C=C double bond. Alkanes do not react with bromine under these conditions, so that this reaction can be used to distinguish between alkanes and alkenes.

Ethene reacts with bromine to form a colourless, saturated product. (Fig 32).

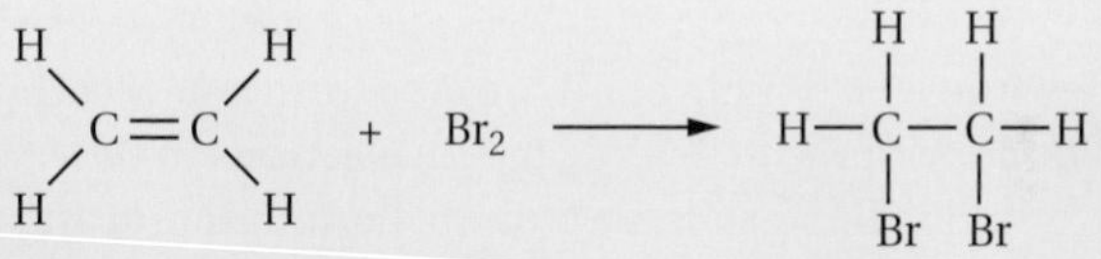

1,2-dibromoethane

Fig 32
Equation for the reaction of ethene with bromine

Examiners' Notes

In aqueous bromine (bromine water), an alternative product, see below, is also formed by attack of the nucleophile water on the carbocation.

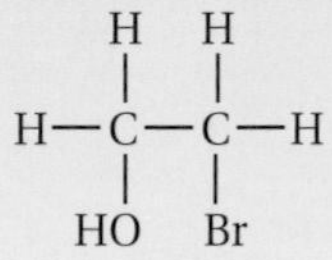

When molecules collide, the electron-rich region of the double bond repels the electrons in the bromine molecule and so induces a dipole in the bromine molecule. The electron-deficient or δ+ bromine atom is the electrophile in the mechanism (see Fig 33).

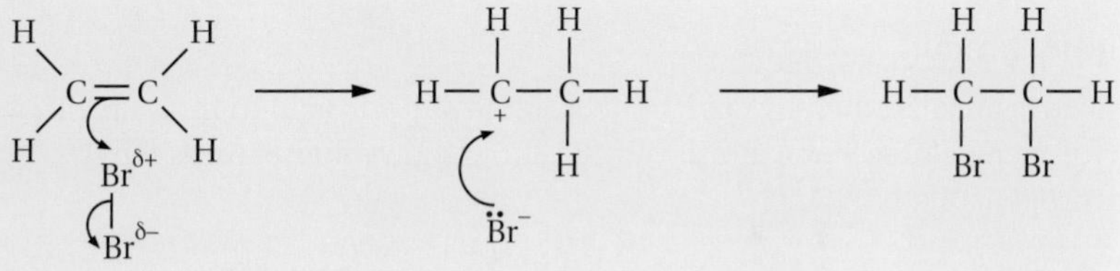

Fig 33
Electrophilic addition mechanism of bromine to ethene

Electrophilic addition reactions to unsymmetrical alkenes

If the alkene is unsymmetrical, such as propene (see Fig 34), and the molecule being added is also unsymmetrical, such as hydrogen bromide (H—Br) or sulfuric acid (H—OSO_2OH), two possible products can form. The major product is the one formed via the *more stable* carbocation.

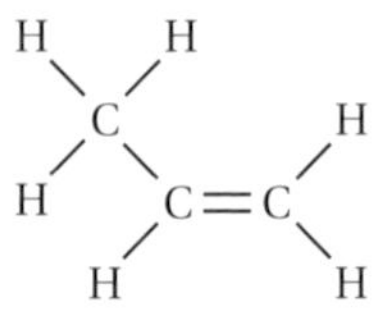

Fig 34
Structure of propene

The order of stability of carbocations is tertiary (3°) > secondary (2°) > primary (1°), owing, to the inductive (electron-releasing) effect of the attached alkyl groups. The more alkyl groups around the carbocation, the more stable it is and the more likely it is to be formed.

The carbocations of $C_4H_9^+$ can have four possible structures (see Fig 35).

primary		secondary		tertiary
$CH_3CH_2CH_2\overset{+}{C}H_2$ $(CH_3)_2CH\overset{+}{C}H_2$	<	$CH_3CH_2\overset{+}{C}HCH_3$	<	$(CH_3)_3\overset{+}{C}$

increasing stability of carbocations →

Fig 35
Possible structures of $C_4H_9^+$

Examiners' Notes

A primary carbocation has one alkyl group attached to C^+.

A secondary carbocation has two alkyl groups attached to C^+.

A tertiary carbocation has three alkyl groups attached to C^+.

Propene reacts with hydrogen bromide to form mostly a secondary carbocation. This species then reacts with the bromide ion to produce 2-bromopropane (see Fig 36).

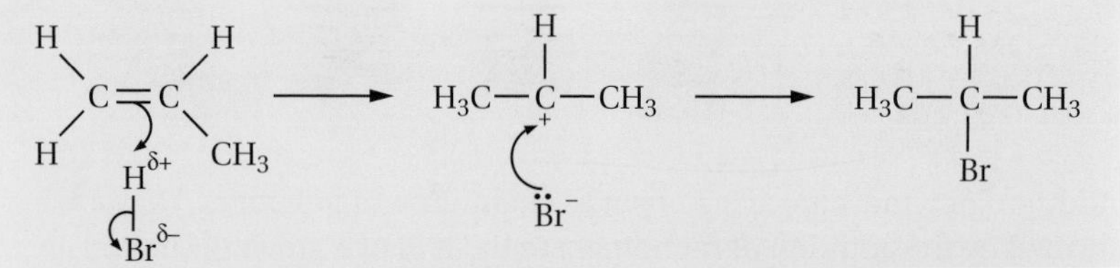

Overall equation: $H_2C{=}CHCH_3 + HBr \longrightarrow CH_3CHBrCH_3$
2-bromopropane

Fig 36
Mechanism of the reaction of propene with hydrogen bromide to form 2-bromopropane, the major product

A little 1-bromopropane will also be formed as the minor product via the less stable primary carbocation, by the mechanism shown in Fig 37.

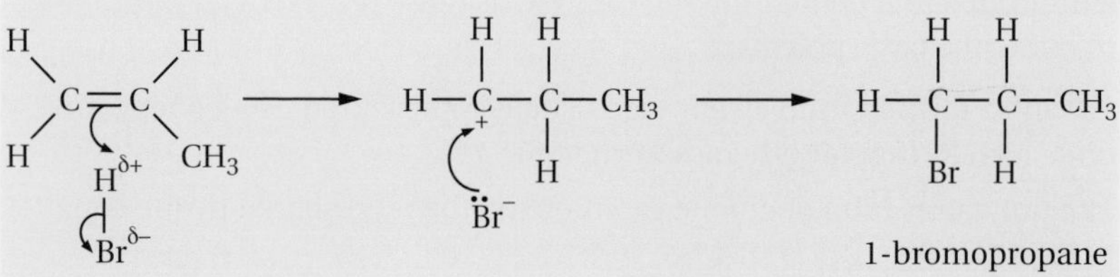

1-bromopropane

Fig 37
Formation of 1-bromopropane, the minor product

The reaction of propene with concentrated sulfuric acid produces mainly 2-propyl hydrogensulfate, via the secondary carbocation. Hydrolysis of this hydrogensulfate forms propan-2-ol (see Fig 38).

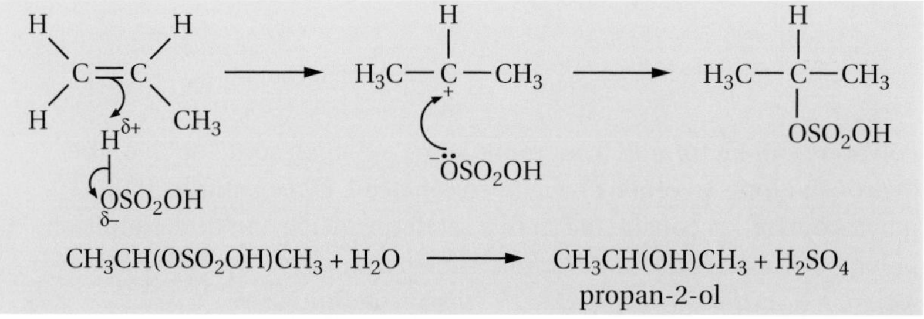

$CH_3CH(OSO_2OH)CH_3 + H_2O \longrightarrow CH_3CH(OH)CH_3 + H_2SO_4$
propan-2-ol

Fig 38
Reaction of propene with concentrated sulfuric acid

Direct hydration of ethene

Ethene reacts with steam at a temperature of 300 °C and a pressure of 6.5×10^3 kPa, in the presence of phosphoric acid (H_3PO_4) as catalyst, to form ethanol by the reaction shown in Fig 39. This reaction illustrates the industrial production of alcohols by the hydration of alkenes in the presence of an acid catalyst.

Essential Notes

6.5×10^3 kPa = 6.5 MPa = 65 bar

Essential Notes

See section 3.2.10 for the production of ethanol by fermentation.

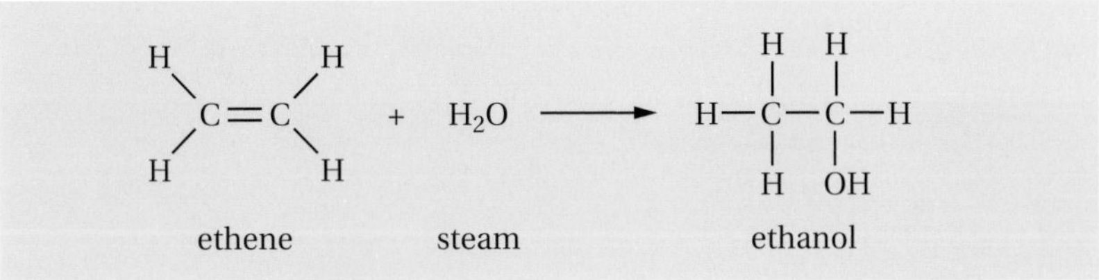

Fig 39
Production of ethanol by the hydration of ethene

Examiners' Notes

The bond energies of C=C and C—C bonds are 612 and 348 kJ mol^{-1}, respectively. Polymerisation, which involves forming two C—C bonds from one C=C bond, is therefore an exothermic process.

Polymerisation of alkenes

Alkene molecules link together in the presence of a catalyst to form addition polymers which are saturated, such as poly(ethene). A section of the polymer (formed from eight ethene molecules) is shown in Fig 40.

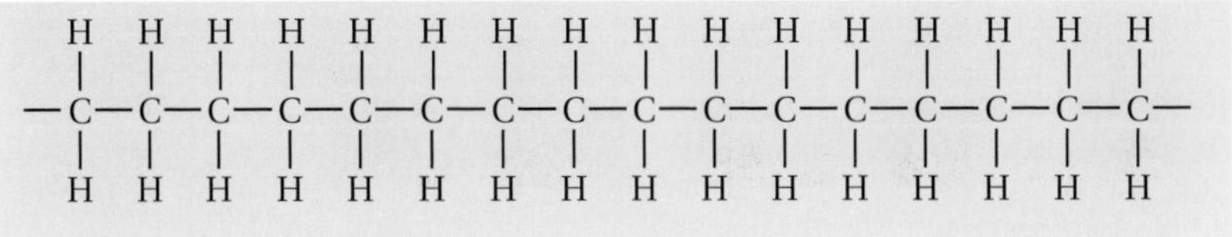

Fig 40
Structure of poly(ethene)

Addition polymers are also known as chain-growth polymers. They are formed by the addition of monomers to the end of a growing chain. The end of the chain is reactive because it is a radical which is formed at the beginning of the reaction by use of catalysts such as organic peroxides, i.e. ROOR. Peroxide molecules readily split into radicals to initiate the chain growth. A radical re-forms at the end of the chain after each addition of a monomer molecule. It is usual to ignore any consideration of the end-groups that come from the catalyst, as these represent an insignificant fraction of a large polymer.

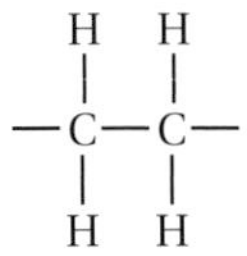

Polymers formed from alkenes are usually represented using a repeating unit, such as that for ethene shown in Fig 41.

Fig 41
The repeating unit of poly(ethene)

The polymerisation of ethene can therefore be represented by the equation in Fig 42.

Examiners' Notes

n represents a large whole number, which is the number of individual molecules (monomers) joining together to form the polymer.

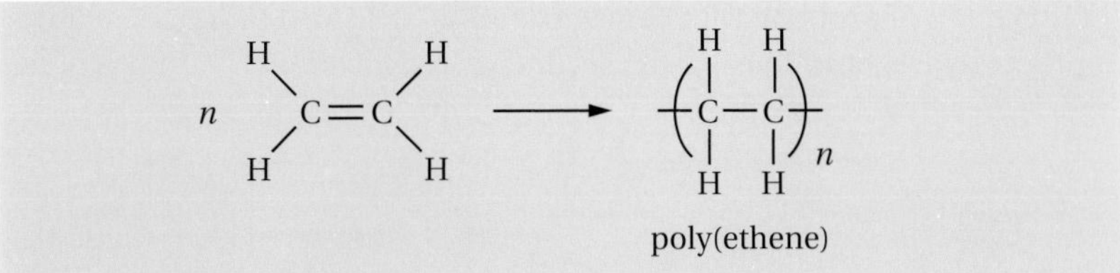

Fig 42
The formation of poly(ethene)

poly(ethene)

Polymers can be formed from monomers, in which some or all of the hydrogen atoms in ethene have been replaced. One example of this, poly(propene), is considered in this section (see Fig 43); other addition polymers are considered in *Collins Student Support Materials: Unit 4 – Kinetics, Equilibria and organic chemistry*, section 3.4.9.

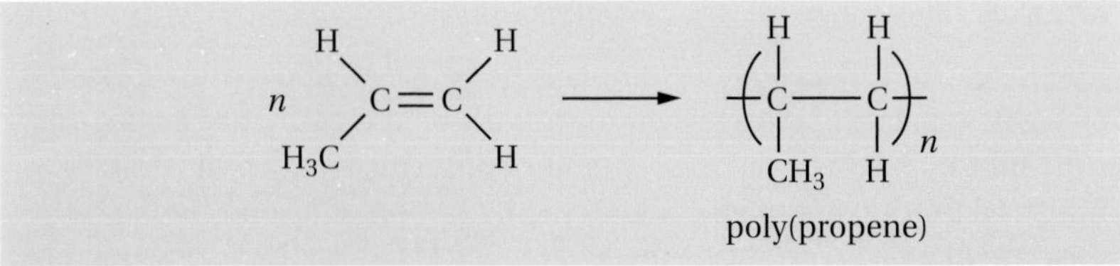

Fig 43
Formation of poly(propene)

poly(propene)

Unlike alkenes, polyalkenes are saturated and therefore are unreactive, like simple alkanes, owing to strong covalent bonds between atoms and a lack of bond polarity. Polyalkenes are also non-biodegradable. However, polymers of this kind are, nevertheless, highly flammable. Methods of disposal of polymers are considered in *Collins Student Support Materials: Unit 4 – Kinetics, Equilibria and Organic chemistry*, section 3.4.9.

Poly(ethene) is used as packaging, especially as thin film and as 'plastic' bags.

Poly(propene) is very versatile. It is used to make rigid containers and objects such as car bumpers. It can also be made into fibres which are used as the backing for carpets and in thermal clothing.

Some polymers, such as poly(propene), can be recycled. Containers made of poly(propene) are collected, cleaned and cut into small pieces. The plastic is then melted and remoulded into a new object or extruded and spun into fibres.

3.2.10 Alcohols

Nomenclature

The alcohols are the homologous series with the general formula $C_nH_{2n+1}OH$. They all contain the functional group, –OH, which is called the hydroxyl group. The first two alcohols are:

- methanol CH_3OH
- ethanol CH_3CH_2OH.

This section also includes three other homologous series of organic compounds: aldehydes, ketones and carboxylic acids; these compounds all contain the carbonyl group $C=O$. The naming of these compounds is illustrated in Table 14 and follows the same rules as were explained in Section 3.1.5.

Homologous series	Name: prefix or suffix	Functional group	Example
alcohols	suffix -ol prefix hydroxy-	—OH	ethanol CH_3CH_2OH 2-hydroxy-propanoic acid $CH_3CH(OH)COOH$
aldehydes	suffix -al	$-C\overset{O}{\underset{H}{\diagup\hspace{-0.5em}\diagdown}}$	ethanal CH_3CHO
ketones	suffix -one prefix oxo-	$C=O$	propanone CH_3COCH_3 3-oxobutanoic acid CH_3COCH_2COOH
carboxylic acids	suffix -oic acid	$-C\overset{O}{\underset{OH}{\diagup\hspace{-0.5em}\diagdown}}$	ethanoic acid CH_3COOH

Table 14
Alcohols, carbonyl compounds and carboxylic acids

Essential Notes

The most common alcohol is ethanol, which is present in 'alcoholic' drinks.

Essential Notes

Fermentation produces an aqueous solution of ethanol at a concentration of between 3% and 15%. Beers usually contain about 3–7% ethanol and wines about 9–15%. Fermentation rarely produces higher concentrations of ethanol because high alcohol concentrations kill the yeast. More concentrated solutions in spirits such as whisky, brandy or gin, which are about 40% ethanol, are made by distillation of the fermented products.

Table 15
Comparison of methods used to produce ethanol

Ethanol production

Fermentation

Alcohol is produced by the process of fermentation, which uses living yeast cells to convert sugars such as glucose into ethanol and carbon dioxide:

$$C_6H_{12}O_6 \xrightarrow{\text{yeast}} 2C_2H_5OH + 2CO_2$$

At low temperatures the reaction is slow, as the enzymes (natural catalysts) in yeast are inactivated; at high temperatures, the yeast cannot survive. The process is therefore normally carried out at a compromise temperature of about 35 °C.

Direct hydration

Ethanol is also produced industrially by the direct hydration of ethene using steam and a phosphoric acid catalyst at 300 °C and 6.5×10^3 kPa pressure (see also section 3.2.9):

$$C_2H_4(g) + H_2O(g) \rightleftharpoons C_2H_5OH(g)$$

Direct hydration is currently preferred for the production of ethanol for industrial use in the UK. However, as this method uses ethene as a raw material, it may become less popular compared to fermentation when oil supplies begin to run out. Table 15 compares the two methods of production.

Method	Rate of reaction	Quality of product	Raw material	Type of process
hydration	fast	pure	ethene from oil (a finite resource)	continuous (cheap on manpower) (expensive equipment)
fermentation	slow	impure	sugars (a renewable resource)	batch (expensive on manpower) (cheap equipment)

Ethanol produced by fermentation is called a **biofuel**. Such a fuel is produced from plants or biomass (material derived from plants), which is renewable because the plant can be grown again quickly. These fuels contrast with fossil fuels, which took millions of years to form and are not renewable.

Combustion of any carbon-containing fuel will eventually increase the amount of carbon dioxide in the atmosphere. However, ethanol as a biofuel can be considered to be **carbon neutral**. This is because the amount of carbon dioxide produced in its combustion, added to the carbon dioxide released during its formation by fermentation, equals the amount of carbon dioxide removed from the atmosphere during photosynthesis, which produces the sugars used in the fermentation that produces the ethanol (see Table 16).

Removal of carbon dioxide from the atmosphere	Release of carbon dioxide into the atmosphere
Photosynthesis	*Fermentation*
$6CO_2 + 6H_2O \rightarrow C_6H_{12}O_6 + 6O_2$	$C_6H_{12}O_6 \rightarrow 2C_2H_5OH + 2CO_2$
6 mol of CO_2 removed per 1 mol of sugar formed	2 mol of CO_2 released per 1 mol of sugar fermented
	Combustion
	$2C_2H_5OH + 6O_2 \rightarrow 4CO_2 + 6H_2O$
	4 mol of CO_2 released during the combustion of the 2 mol of ethanol formed per 1 mol of sugar fermented
Total: 6 moles of CO₂ removed	**Total: 6 moles of CO₂ released**

Table 16
Carbon-neutral status of ethanol produced by fermentation

Examiners' Notes

Although Table 16 seems to indicate that ethanol can be considered to be carbon neutral, the production and processing steps require energy. The production of this energy may involve the release of additional carbon dioxide.

However, there are concerns about the increased production of bioethanol and similar fuels. The land area used to grow crops suitable for fermentation may increase and can lead to further deforestation (as in the Amazon basin). Trees act as a natural 'store' of carbon dioxide, but this carbon dioxide is released after deforestation when timber is burned. Also, the use of land to grow crops to produce these fuels in developing countries has already reduced the land available for growing crops for much-needed food.

Classifications and reactions

Alcohols can be classified as primary, secondary or tertiary, depending on the carbon skeleton to which the hydroxyl group is attached, as shown in Fig 44, where R is any alkyl group.

Many reactions of the OH functional group are the same in all alcohols, independent of where the OH group is attached to the carbon skeleton. However, the three types of alcohol differ in their reactions with oxidising agents such as acidified potassium dichromate(VI).

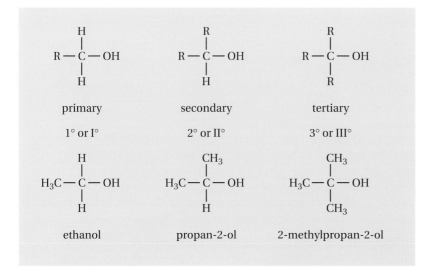

Fig 44
Classification of alcohols
(R represents any alkyl group)

Oxidation of alcohols

Primary alcohols are oxidised first to aldehydes, such as ethanal, as shown in Fig 45.

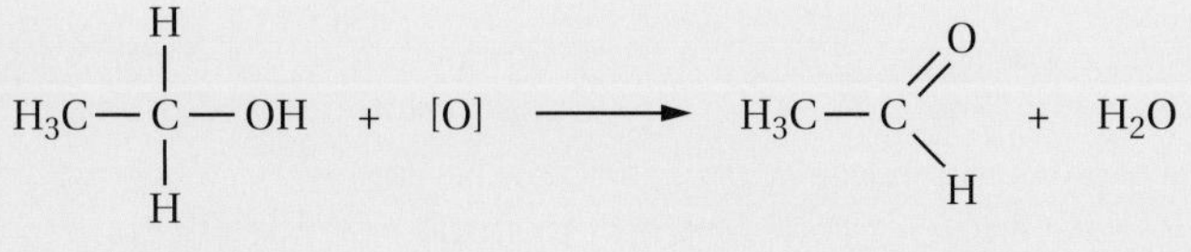

Fig 45
Oxidation of ethanol

ethanol   ethanal

Examiners' Notes

The use of [O] to represent the oxidant is an allowed simplification in this and other equations showing the oxidation of organic compounds. The equations, however, must still balance.

An aldehyde still has one hydrogen atom attached to the carbonyl carbon, and so it can be oxidised one step further to a carboxylic acid (see Fig 46).

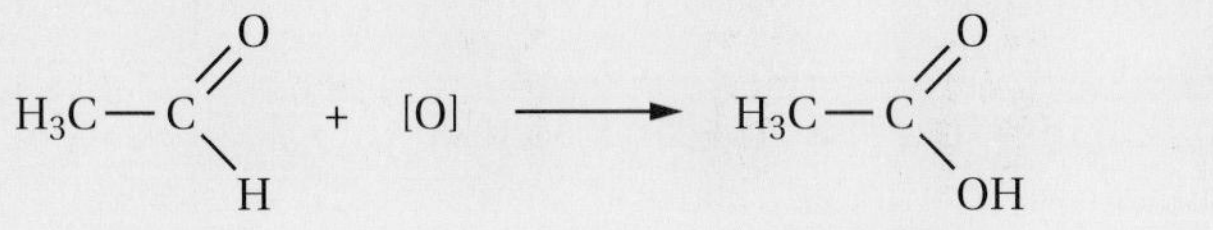

ethanal   ethanoic acid

Fig 46
Oxidation of ethanal

In practice, a primary alcohol such as ethanol is dripped into a warm solution of acidified potassium dichromate(VI). The aldehyde, ethanal, is formed and immediately distils off, thereby preventing further oxidation to ethanoic acid, because the boiling point of ethanal (23 °C) is much lower than that of either the original alcohol ethanol (78 °C) or of ethanoic acid (118 °C). Both the alcohol and the acid have higher boiling points because of hydrogen bonding.

Essential Notes

Alcoholic drinks such as wine and beer that are left exposed to air go sour. This is because the ethanol present is oxidised to ethanoic acid by oxygen using enzymes from bacteria. However, the bacteria cannot tolerate ethanol concentrations greater than about 20%, so the ethanol in high alcohol drinks is not oxidised. This applies to all spirits and also to fortified wines such as sherry and port.

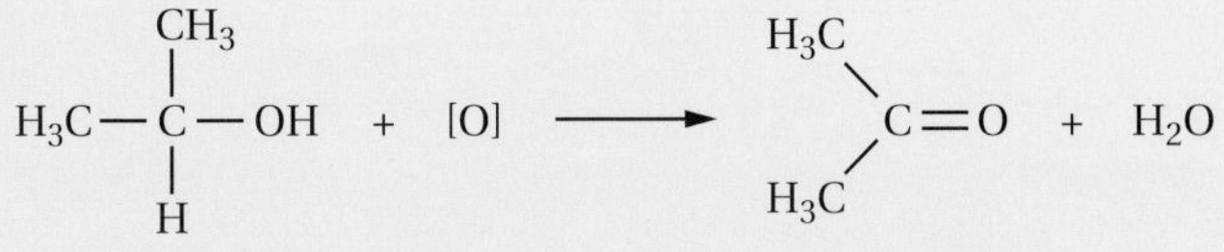

If oxidation of ethanol to ethanoic acid is required, the reagents must be heated together under **reflux** to prevent escape of the aldehyde before it can be oxidised further.

Secondary alcohols are oxidised to ketones (see Fig 47). These have no hydrogen atoms attached to the carbonyl carbon and so cannot easily be oxidised further.

propan-2-ol   propanone

Fig 47
Oxidation of propan-2-ol

When orange potassium dichromate(VI) in acidified solution acts as an oxidising agent, it is reduced to green chromium(III) ions. Primary and secondary alcohols both turn the solution from an orange to a green when they are oxidised, and this colour change can be used to distinguish them from tertiary alcohols. Tertiary alcohols are not oxidised by acidified dichromate(VI) ions, so they have no effect on its colour, which remains orange.

Essential Notes

Tertiary alcohols are not easily oxidised.

Distinguishing between aldehydes and ketones

The reaction with acidified potassium dichromate(VI) distinguishes between tertiary alcohols on the one hand, and primary and secondary alcohols on the other, but cannot distinguish between primary and secondary alcohols. However, these can be differentiated by further tests on their oxidation products. Aldehydes formed from primary alcohols are easily oxidised to carboxylic acids, but ketones formed from secondary alcohols are not easily oxidised. Observing whether or not further oxidation occurs can therefore be used to differentiate between them.

Although ketones are not easily oxidised, they react with powerful oxidising agents causing carbon–carbon bonds to break and forming mixtures of carboxylic acids. Any distinguishing reaction must therefore use *mild* oxidising agents to prevent this bond-breaking from occurring. The following are two such examples:

- **Tollens' reagent** contains the complex ion $[Ag(NH_3)_2]^+$ and is prepared by adding a slight excess of aqueous ammonia to silver nitrate solution. When gently warmed, aldehydes reduce this complex ion and produce a silver mirror on the walls of a test tube; ketones do not form a silver mirror.

- **Fehling's solution** contains a deep blue copper(II) complex ion which on warming is reduced by aldehydes, but not by ketones, to form a red precipitate of copper(I) oxide, Cu_2O.

When aldehydes act as reducing agents in these reactions, they are oxidised to carboxylic acids as shown by the equation:

$$RCHO + [O] \rightarrow RCOOH$$

Elimination

Alcohols with a hydrogen atom on the carbon next to the OH group can be dehydrated to alkenes when heated to about 180 °C with concentrated sulfuric or concentrated phosphoric acid. The reaction is an acid-catalysed elimination. Details of the mechanism are not required in this specification.

Examples of such elimination reactions are shown in Figs 48–50.

Essential Notes

If a large excess of ammonia is used, this reacts with the aldehyde leaving none to react with the $[Ag(NH_3)_2]^+$ ion. Hence, a silver mirror will not be seen.

Examiners' Notes

Some alcohols may form more than one alkene on dehydration, e.g. butan-2-ol can form but-1-ene and but-2-ene (see also elimination from haloalkanes in section 3.2.8).

Fig 48
Dehydration of ethanol

$$H_3C-CH_2OH \longrightarrow H_2C{=}CH_2 + H_2O$$

ethanol   ethene

Fig 49
Dehydration of propan-2-ol

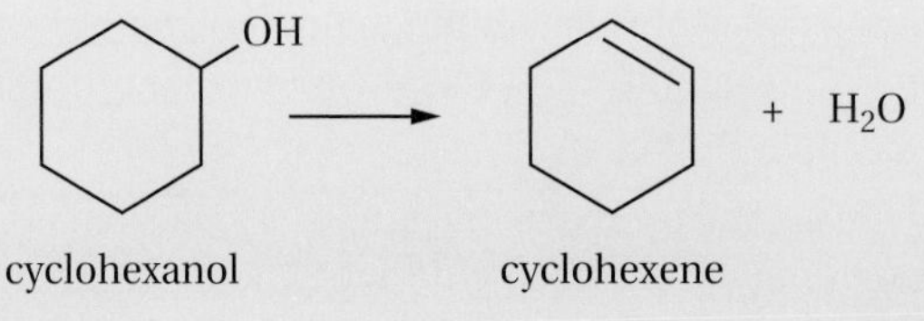

$$H_3C-CH-CH_3 \longrightarrow H_2C{=}CH-CH_3 + H_2O$$
$$\qquad\quad |$$
$$\qquad\ OH$$

propan-2-ol   propene

Fig 50
Dehydration of cyclohexanol

cyclohexanol   cyclohexene

The alkenes produced, such as ethene and propene, can be used as the starting materials (monomers) in addition polymerisation reactions (see section 3.2.9). Hence, this dehydration reaction provides an alternative route to addition polymers compared with the usual method starting from oil. The two routes are:

$$\text{alcohols} \xrightarrow{\text{dehydration}} \text{alkenes} \longrightarrow \text{polymers}$$

$$\text{crude oil} \xrightarrow[\text{distillation}]{\text{fractional}} \text{alkanes} \xrightarrow{\text{cracking}} \text{alkenes} \longrightarrow \text{polymers}$$

The route from alcohols may use renewable starting materials, whereas production from crude oil uses up vital natural resources.

3.2.11 Analytical techniques

The main analytical techniques used to determine the structures of organic compounds are mass spectrometry and infra-red spectroscopy (discussed in this section), and nuclear magnetic resonance spectroscopy (discussed in *Collins Student Support Materials: Unit 4 – Kinetics, Equilibria and Organic Chemistry*, section 3.4.11). These techniques are often used in combination.

Examiners' Notes

Note that the species $M^{+\bullet}$ formed in a mass spectrometer is a cation and also a radical, because a covalent bond has lost one of its two electrons.

Compound	Precise mass
C_6H_{12}	84.093895
C_5H_8O	84.057511
$C_4H_4O_2$	84.021127
$C_4H_8N_2$	84.068744

Table 17
Precise masses of four compounds with $m/z = 84$

Essential Notes

Exercise: Try to work out the nine structural isomers of C_3H_6O, some of which are cyclic.

Mass spectrometry

When a sample of an organic compound (M) is introduced into a mass spectrometer, provided that the molecule is not completely fragmented the peak at the maximum value of m/z (see *Collins Student Support Materials: Unit 1 – Foundation Chemistry*, section 3.1.1) corresponds to the **molecular ion, $M^{+\bullet}$**. The value of m/z for this ion is equal to the relative molecular mass (M_r).

Many organic molecules have the same **integral mass**. Thus, for example, to the nearest integer, the relative molecular masses of C_6H_{12}, C_5H_8O, $C_4H_4O_2$ and $C_4H_8N_2$ are identical ($M_r = 84$). However, if more precise relative atomic masses are used, slightly different M_r values are obtained for these molecules (see Table 17).

High-resolution mass spectrometers are capable of measuring the precise m/z of any molecular ion. By comparing this experimental value with that calculated for each species having the same integral mass, it is possible to assign a molecular formula to an unknown ion. Modern high-resolution instruments possess computer programs designed to match precise masses with molecular formulae. It needs to be appreciated, of course, that a particular molecular formula, although unambiguous, can represent many isomers. For example, C_3H_6O is the molecular formula of nine different structural isomers.

Mass spectra reveal the presence of isotopes. Of particular interest are molecules containing bromine or chlorine, where two isotopes are present in substantial quantities. The ratio of the relative isotopic abundances of ^{35}Cl (75.8%) and ^{37}Cl (24.2%) is close to 3:1. Thus, for example, the mass spectra of monochloroalkanes exhibit molecular ions two mass units apart in a 3:1 intensity ratio due to the presence of $R^{35}Cl$ and $R^{37}Cl$, respectively.

Similarly, the mass spectra of monobromoalkanes show molecular ion peaks two mass units apart in a near to 1:1 intensity ratio, because ^{79}Br (50.7%) in R^{79}Br and ^{81}Br (49.3%) in R^{81}Br have approximately the same abundance (Fig 51). These distinctive features are helpful in revealing the presence of chlorine or bromine.

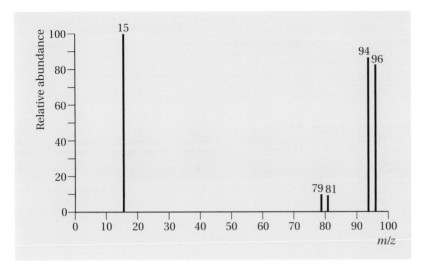

Fig 51
Simplified mass spectrum of bromomethane, CH$_3$Br

Infra-red spectroscopy

The entire infra-red spectrum of an organic compound provides a unique **molecular fingerprint**. Thus, if two samples have identical infra-red spectra, the compounds must be identical. Also, comparison can be made between the full infra-red spectrum of a pure material and the full spectrum of a sample, when the presence of any impurities will show up as extra peaks.

Of more general use is the *identification of functional groups* in organic compounds. Most functional groups give rise to characteristic infra-red absorptions which change little from one compound to another.

Absorption of infra-red energy by a molecule causes *bond stretching* and *bond bending*, giving rise to the appearance of peaks at particular **wavenumbers**. The position of an infra-red peak depends on the bond strength and on the masses of the atoms which are joined by the bond. Since bending involves less energy than stretching, for the same bonds, bending absorptions occur at lower wavenumbers than stretching modes. Strong bonds and light atoms vibrate at relatively high wavenumbers. Conversely, weak bonds and heavy atoms absorb at lower wavenumbers.

It is convenient to divide the infra-red spectrum into four regions for purposes of structure interpretation (see Table 18).

Examiners' Notes

Frequency (f) is related to wavelength (λ) by the expression $f = c/\lambda$, where c is the speed of light; f is given in Hz (s^{-1}). By convention, however, infra-red band positions are quoted as reciprocal wavelengths ($1/\lambda$), alternatively called wavenumbers, with units cm^{-1}. wavenumbers are directly related to energy ($E = hf$, where h is the Planck constant).

Essential Notes

The wavenumber range 400 to 4000 cm^{-1} corresponds to an absorption of energy between 4.8 and 48 kJ mol^{-1}. The energy involved is much less than that required to break covalent bonds.

Table 18
Regions in the infra-red spectrum

Region/cm^{-1}	Absorptions
4000–2500	C–H, O–H, N–H
2500–2000	C≡C, C≡N
2000–1500	C=C, C=O, C=N
1500–400	C–C, C–O, C–N, C–X

The region below 1500 cm^{-1} is the **fingerprint region**, which is often complex owing to a wide variety of single-bond vibrations. Nearly all organic molecules absorb strongly close to 3000 cm^{-1}, owing to C—H stretching vibrations associated with alkyl groups. The position of the C—H stretch is shifted by the presence of adjacent multiple bonds (see Table 19). The aldehyde C—H stretch is distinctive.

Table 19
Some characteristic infra-red absorptions due to bond stretching in organic molecules

Bond	Types of compound	Range/cm^{-1}
C–H	alkanes	2850–2960
	alkenes	3010–3095
	alkynes	3250–3300
	arenes	3030–3080
	aldehydes	2710–2730
O–H	alcohols (H-bonded)	3230–3550
	carboxylic acids (H-bonded)	2500–3000
N–H	amines	3320–3560
C–C	alkanes	750–1100
C=C	alkenes	1620–1680
C≡C	alkynes	2100–2250
C–O	alcohols, ethers, carboxylic acids, esters	1000–1300
C=O	aldehydes, ketones, carboxylic acids, esters	1680–1750
C–N	amines	1180–1360
C≡N	nitriles	2210–2260
C–Cl	haloalkanes	600–800
C–Br	haloalkanes	500–600

Examiners' Notes

Note that appropriate infra-red data will be provided in examination questions and on the reverse side of the Periodic Table provided.

Carbonyl containing compounds show a very characteristic strong absorption in the range 1600–1800 cm^{-1}, the actual value of which depends on the nature of the adjacent groups. For example, simple aldehydes and ketones absorb at about 1720 cm^{-1}, whereas esters are closer to 1740 cm^{-1}. Owing to hydrogen bonding, hydroxyl groups tend to have broad O—H absorption bands around 3300 cm^{-1}; carboxylic acid groups have very broad O—H bands in the region of 3000 cm^{-1}.

The examination of an infra-red absorption spectrum is a useful way of identifying particular functional groups, especially when used in conjunction with mass spectrometry or nuclear magnetic resonance spectroscopy. It is important to appreciate that much structural information can be derived from an infra-red spectrum by noticing which characteristic absorptions are *absent*.

Examiners' Notes

Absorptions due to various kinds of C—H bending in saturated groups appear characteristically at about 1460 cm^{-1} and 1370 cm^{-1}.

Illustrative infra-red absorption spectra are shown for propan-2-ol (Fig 52), propanal (Fig 53) and propanoic acid (Fig 54). Real samples are rarely perfect and often contain trace amounts of water. In such cases, weak absorptions in the O—H region can be observed (see Fig 53).

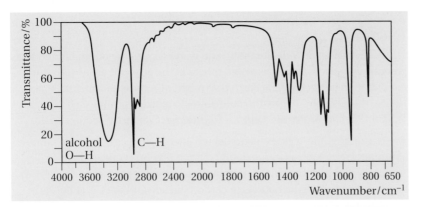

Fig 52
Infra-red spectrum of propan-2-ol,
$(CH_3)_2CHOH$

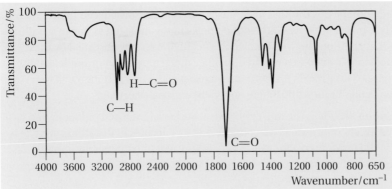

Fig 53
Infra-red spectrum of propanal,
CH_3CH_2CHO

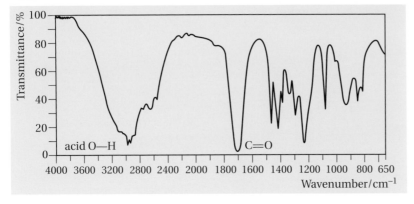

Fig 54
Infra-red spectrum of propanoic
acid, CH_3CH_2COOH

Absorption of infra-red radiation and global warming

The gases carbon dioxide, methane and water vapour are often referred to as **greenhouse gases**. These gases and others in the atmosphere absorb infra red radiation emitted by the Earth that might otherwise escape into space. Hence, the gases are thought to contribute to global warming (see *Collins Student Support Materials: Unit 1 – Foundation Chemistry*, section 3.1.6).

The reason that these gases have such an effect, whereas other, much more abundant gases such as nitrogen and oxygen do not, is due to their structures and the bonds they contain. The vibrational energies of the O—H bonds in water, the C=O bonds in carbon dioxide and the C—H bonds in methane correspond to energies in the infra-red region. When infra-red radiation passes through these gases, energy is absorbed (see Table 19) and these bonds stretch and the bond angles in the molecules change (bending). When collisions between molecules occur, the energy absorbed by these molecules can be a transferred to other molecules as, for example, kinetic energy. This process results in an increase in the average energy of the molecules in the atmosphere and, hence, global warming.

Carbon dioxide is the most effective absorber of infra-red radiation but, as it comprises only a small percentage of the molecules in the atmosphere, it is not the most important. Water vapour, present in far larger amounts, is responsible for most of the infra-red energy absorbed.

How Science Works

The introduction of the *How Science Works* component into the new A-level specifications has made formal an approach to the teaching of topics in science which many teachers have, in fact, already been using.

Irrespective of future careers, science students need to become proficient in dealing with the various issues included in *How Science Works* so as to achieve a level of scientific awareness. In order to gain an appreciation of how chemists, in particular, work (using the scientific method) it is necessary to understand and be able to apply the concepts, principles and theories of chemistry. The ways that chemical theories and laws are developed, together with the potential impact of new discoveries on society in general, should become clear to you as new concepts in the specification are explored.

Science starts with experimental observation and investigation, followed by verification (i.e. confirmation by others that the results are reliable). A theory or model is proposed to try to explain a set of observations, which may themselves have been accidental or planned as part of a series of experiments. During A-level chemistry courses, many different types of experiment will be carried out and evaluated.

Once an initial theory, or hypothesis, has been put forward to explain a set of results, further experiments are carried out to test the ability of this theory to make accurate predictions. An initial theory may need to be adapted to take into account fresh evidence. More observations and experimental results are produced and the cycle is continued until a firm theory can be established. It is very important that all experiments are carried out objectively, without any bias towards a desired result.

A-level Chemistry courses provide various opportunities for students to analyse verified experimental data as well as the chance to develop theories based on novel findings. In some instances, it will be recognised that there is insufficient experimental evidence for a firm theory to be accepted. In other cases, different experiments carried out by different people will produce contradictory results. Sometimes an apparently unusual result or observation, if verified, will be of great significance. There then follow opportunities to debate these issues and to understand how conflicting theories can be resolved by the accumulation of further evidence.

The concepts and principles dealt with under *How Science Works* will be assessed during the examination. The questions set will require only a knowledge and understanding of the topics included in the specification. In some instances, however, the ability to analyse and make deductions from unfamiliar information may be required. Typical examination questions are provided at the end of the unit and aspects of *How Science Works* are highlighted.

Practice exam-style questions

1 (a) What is meant by the term *enthalpy change?*

_____

_____ 2 marks

(b) Define the term *standard enthalpy of formation.*

_____

_____

_____ 3 marks

(c) (i) Use the mean bond enthalpy data given in the table below to calculate the enthalpy change for the
following reaction.

$$C_3H_8(g) + 5O_2(g) \rightarrow 3CO_2(g) + 4H_2O(g)$$

	C—C	C—H	O=O	C=O	O—H
Mean bond enthalpy/kJ mol^{-1}	348	412	496	743	463

_____

_____

_____

(ii) The enthalpy change for this reaction can also be calculated by using the standard enthalpies of formation
of the reactants and the products.

Explain why the value obtained by using mean bond enthalpies is likely to be less accurate than the value
obtained from enthalpies of formation.

_____

_____

(iii) State how the enthalpy change for the reaction given in (c)(i) would differ if the water formed in the
reaction were a liquid rather than a gas. Explain your answer.

How enthalpy change would differ _____

_____

Explanation _____

_____

_____ 7 marks

Total Marks: 12

2 **(a)** Define the term *activation energy.*

_____

_____ 2 marks

(b) Explain why a small increase in temperature can result in a large increase in the rate of a chemical reaction.

_____

_____ 2 marks

(c) Explain why a small increase in the concentration of a reactant can result in a small increase in the rate of a reaction.

_____

_____

_____ 2 marks

(d) Explain why the addition of a catalyst can result in an increase in the rate of a reaction.

_____

_____

_____ 2 marks

Total Marks: 8

3 A chemical production plant manufactures methanol by the reaction between carbon monoxide and hydrogen as indicated by the equation below.

$$CO(g) + 2H_2(g) \rightleftharpoons CH_3OH(g) \quad \Delta H^\ominus = -201 \text{ kJ mol}^{-1}$$

As a result of an increase in the demand for methanol, the plant manager was asked to change the operating conditions in order to increase the amount of methanol produced each day.

(a) The use of a catalyst was suggested.

Explain why this change would not affect the equilibrium yield but would enable the daily production of methanol to be increased.

_____

_____

_____ 3 marks

(b) An increase in the operating temperature of the plant was suggested.

(i) State how an increase in temperature would affect the equilibrium yield and explain your answer.

Effect on yield _____

_____

Explanation ——————————————————————————————————————

——

(ii) Explain the factors that determine the final choice of operating temperature.

——

——

—— 6 marks

(c) An increase in the operating pressure for the process was suggested.

State two advantages and two disadvantages of using an increased pressure.

Advantages ——

——

Disadvantages ——

————————————————————————————————————— 4 marks

Total Marks: 13

4 **(a)** By referring to electrons, define the term *oxidation*.

———————————————————————————————————— 1 mark

(b) The following reaction occurs when sulfur dioxide, SO_2, is bubbled through an acidified solution containing VO_3^- ions.

$$2VO_3^- + SO_2 + 4H^+ \rightarrow 2VO^{2+} + SO_4^{2-} + 2H_2O$$

(i) Deduce the oxidation state of V in VO_3^- and that in VO^{2+}.

VO_3^- ——————————————————————————————————————

VO^{2+} ——————————————————————————————————————

(ii) Identify the reducing agent in the reaction above and write a half-equation for the oxidation of this reducing agent.

Reducing agent ————————————————————————————————————

Half-equation —————————————————————————————————5 marks

(c) In acidic solution, zinc reduces VO_3^- to V^{2+} and the zinc is itself oxidised to Zn^{2+}.

(i) Deduce a half-equation for the reduction of VO_3^- to V^{2+}.

——

(ii) Use this half-equation to construct an overall equation for the reduction, in acid solution, of VO_3^- to V^{2+} by zinc.

———————————————————————————————————— 3 marks

Total Marks: 9

5 (a) An aqueous solution containing bromide ions is added to one test-tube and an aqueous solution containing iodide ions is added to a second test-tube. By stating the observations you would make, explain how these two solutions could be distinguished by using

(i) an aqueous solution of chlorine

_____

_____

_____

(ii) an aqueous solution of silver nitrate followed by a concentrated solution of aqueous ammonia.

_____

_____

_____

_____ 6 marks

(b) By stating the observations you would make, explain how concentrated sulfuric acid can be used to distinguish between solid samples of sodium chloride and sodium bromide. Write an overall equation for a reaction with either of these halides that occurs without any change in oxidation state, and also an equation that represents a redox reaction.

Observation(s) with NaCl _____

_____

Observation(s) with NaBr _____

_____

Without redox _____

Redox _____ 6 marks

Total Marks: 12

6 (a) State and explain the trend in the first ionisation energies of the Group 2 elements from Mg to Ba.

Trend _____

Explanation _____

_____ 3 marks

(b) By stating the observations you would make, explain how the addition of aqueous sodium hydroxide would enable you to distinguish between an aqueous solution containing magnesium ions and one containing barium ions. Write an ionic equation for any reaction that occurs.

Observation(s) with Mg^{2+} ions _____

_____

Observation(s) with Ba^{2+} ions _____

_____

Equation _____ 3 marks

(c) Lime kilns have long been used as a first step in the production of calcium hydroxide, Ca(OH)$_2$, from calcium carbonate, CaCO$_3$. Limestone, which consists mainly of calcium carbonate, is partially decomposed by heat to form calcium oxide, CaO. Calcium hydroxide is formed from this product when water is added. Explain why calcium hydroxide is important in agriculture.

_____

_____ 2 marks

(d) Barium sulfate is used in medicine even though reference books state that barium compounds are very toxic. Give a medical use of barium sulfate and explain why this barium compound is not toxic.

Use of barium sulfate _____

_____

Explanation _____

_____ 2 marks

Total Marks: 10

7 Metallic elements are often found in the Earth's crust combined with either oxygen or sulfur. The first step in the extraction of a metal from a sulfide ore is usually the conversion of this ore into the oxide.

Extraction of metals from metal oxide ores and their derivatives can be achieved by a number of different methods.

(a) State the major environmental problem associated with the conversion of a sulfide ore into an oxide. Identify the chemical which causes this problem and suggest how the problem can be overcome.

Environmental problem _____

Chemical responsible _____

How problem can be overcome _____

_____ 3 marks

(b) Give three different methods of extracting metals from their ores and, in each case, write an equation for the reaction involved.

Method 1 _____

Equation 1 _____

MILLFIELD SCHOOL
LIBRARY

Method 2 _____

Equation 2 _____

Method 3 _____

Equation 3 _____

_____ 6 marks

Total Marks: 9

8 **(a)** Name and outline a mechanism for the reaction of Cl_2 with CH_2Cl_2 to form $CHCl_3$.

Name of mechanism _____

Mechanism _____

_____

_____ 4 marks

(b) The compound CH_3CHF_2 is one of a series of compounds, known as HFCs, which can be used as replacements for CFCs in refrigerators.

(i) Write an equation for the formation of CH_3CHF_2 from ethane and fluorine.

_____

(ii) Write three equations to illustrate the reactions by which CF_2Cl_2 contributes to the depletion of the ozone layer.

_____

_____

_____

_____

(iii) Explain why HFCs are less harmful to the ozone layer than CFCs.

_____

_____

_____ 6 marks

Total Marks: 10

9 Chemists often wish to synthesise new molecules with longer carbon chains than the starting molecule. One method of adding another carbon atom to a chain uses cyanide ions.

(a) Write an equation for the reaction of bromoethane with potassium cyanide and name the organic product.

_____

_____ 2 marks

(b) Name and outline a mechanism for this reaction.

Name of mechanism _____

Mechanism _____

3 marks

(c) Predict, with a reason, whether the reaction of chloroethane with potassium cyanide would be faster or slower than the reaction in part (a).

_____

_____

_____ 2 marks

Total Marks: 7

10 (a) Draw displayed formulae for the *E* and *Z*–isomers of pent-2-ene. Explain why this type of stereoisomerism occurs.

E–isomer   *Z–isomer*

Explanation _____

_____

_____ 4 marks

(b) The reaction of HBr with but-1-ene produces a pair of structural isomers.

Name and outline the mechanism of the reaction to form the major isomeric product and explain why more of this isomer is formed.

Name of mechanism _____

Mechanism

Explanation _____

_____ 7 marks

Total Marks: 11

11 Under suitable conditions, ethene reacts with steam to produce ethanol in a reversible reaction as shown below.

$$C_2H_4(g) + H_2O(g) \rightleftharpoons C_2H_5OH(g)$$

(a) Given the following values for enthalpies of formation, $\Delta H_f^{\ominus}$, calculate a value for ΔH for this reaction.

Compound	$C_2H_4(g)$	$H_2O(g)$	$C_2H_5OH(g)$
$\Delta H_f^{\ominus}/kJ \, mol^{-1}$	+52.3	−242	−235

_____

_____

_____ 2 marks

(b) Predict the most suitable conditions to produce the maximum yield of ethanol using this reaction and discuss why the conditions used in practice differ from your predictions.

_____

_____

_____

_____

_____ 4 marks

Total Marks: 6

12 (a) Draw the repeating unit of the polymer formed by ethene and the repeating unit of the polymer formed by propene. Name the type of polymerisation involved.

Repeating unit from ethene _____

Repeating unit from propene _____

Type of polymerisation _____ 3 marks

(b) Explain why these two polymers have relatively low melting points.

_____

_____ 2 marks

(c) Explain why it makes commercial sense to recycle objects made from poly(propene) rather than to bury them as household waste.

_____

_____ 2 marks

Total Marks: 7

13 (a) Write an equation to show the formation of ethanol by fermentation of glucose and give the conditions used for this reaction.

Equation _____

Conditions _____

_____ 4 marks

(b) Ethanol is an important solvent in industrial processes. Discuss the advantages and disadvantages of the production of ethanol by fermentation compared with its production by the direct hydration of ethene.

_____

_____

_____

_____ 4 marks

Total Marks: 8

14 (a) Write an equation for the complete combustion of ethanol.

_____ 1 mark

(b) Explain why the use of ethanol as a fuel can be considered to be carbon neutral.

_____

_____

_____

_____

_____

_____

_____ 6 marks

Total Marks: 7

15 (a) Draw and name the four alcohols which are isomers of $C_4H_{10}O$ and classify them as primary, secondary or tertiary.

Structure 1	Structure 2
Name _____	Name _____
Type of alcohol _____	Type of alcohol _____
Structure 3	Structure 4
Name _____	Name _____
Type of alcohol _____	Type of alcohol _____

12 marks

(b) Describe how you could distinguish between the three types of alcohol you have named above using acidified potassium dichromate(VI) solution and also Tollens' solution.

_____

_____

_____

_____ 2 marks

Total Marks: 14

16 (a) Analysis of an organic compound, **X**, showed that its relative molecular mass was 102. This value could arise from several different molecular formulae, including:

(i) $C_4H_6O_3$, (ii) $C_5H_{10}O_2$ and (iii) $C_3H_6N_2O_2$

Analysis of the high-resolution mass spectrum of **X** showed that the molecular ion of this compound produces a peak at $m/z = 102.0678$. Use the precise relative atomic masses given below to deduce which one of the three molecular formulae corresponds to **X** and show that the other two do not.

$$C = 12.0000 \quad H = 1.0078 \quad O = 15.9949 \quad N = 14.0031$$

_____

_____

_____ 3 marks

(b) The infra-red spectrum of **X** is shown below.

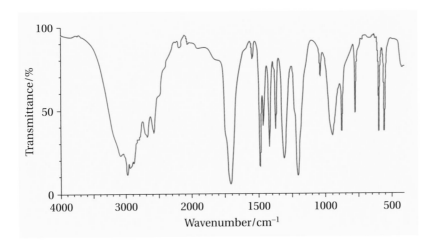

(i) Use the table of infra-red absorptions provided below to identify the functional group present in **X**.

_____

(ii) Draw the structures of the isomers of **X** which contain this functional group.

(iii) Describe how the fingerprint region of the infra-red spectrum could be used to identify which isomer was **X**.

_____

_____ 7 marks

Total Marks: 10

Bond	Wavenumber/cm^{-1}
C – H	2850–3300
C – C	750–1100
C = C	1620–1680
C = O	1680–1750
C – O	1000–1300
O – H (alcohols)	3230–3550
O – H (acids)	2500–3000

Answers, explanations, hints and tips

Question	Answer		Marks
1 (a)	heat energy evolved	(1)	
	at constant pressure	(1)	2
1 (b)	the enthalpy change when one mole of a substance	(1)	
	is formed from its elements		
	with all reactants and products in their standard states	(1)	
	under standard conditions	(1)	3
1 (c) (i)	$\Delta H_r = \Sigma$ enthalpy of bonds broken $- \Sigma$ enthalpy of bonds formed	(1)	
	$= [(2 \times 348) + (8 \times 412) + (5 \times 496)] - [(6 \times 743) + (8 \times 463)]$	(1)	
	$= -1690$ kJ mol^{-1}	(1)	3
1 (c) (ii)	mean bond enthalpies are values averaged over many compounds	(1)	
	so mean bond enthalpies are not exact for specific compounds	(1)	2
1 (c) (iii)	the value would show the reaction to be more exothermic	(1)	
	heat is evolved when molecules attract each other, changing from a gas to a liquid	(1)	2
			Total 12
2 (a)	minimum energy	(1)	
	required for reaction to occur	(1)	2
2 (b)	many more molecules	(1)	
	have energy greater than the activation energy	(1)	2
2 (c)	a small increase in concentration results in a small increase in the frequency of collisions	(1)	
	only a small fraction of collisions has energy greater than the activation energy	(1)	2
2 (d)	provides an alternative route with a lower activation energy	(1)	
	more molecules have energy greater than the activation energy	(1)	2
			Total 8
3 (a)	rates of forward and backward reactions both increased	(1)	
	by an equal amount	(1)	
	but, as equilibrium is achieved in less time, more methanol can be made	(1)	3
3 (b) (i)	equilibrium yield decreases	(1)	
	system tries to lower temperature (opposes change)	(1)	
	so that endothermic (backward) reaction favoured	(1)	3
3 (b) (ii)	increasing temperature increases the rate of the reaction	(1)	
	a compromise temperature is required	(1)	
	balancing equilibrium yield and reaction rate	(1)	3
3 (c)	more methanol produced	(1)	
	increase in sales income	(1)	
	cost of increased pressure	(1)	
	hazards of plant operation	(1)	4
			Total 13

Question	Answer		Marks
4 (a)	the process of electron loss	(1)	1
4 (b) (i)	VO_3^- is +5	(1)	
	V in VO^{2+} is +4	(1)	2
4 (b) (ii)	SO_2	(1)	
	$SO_2 + 2H_2O \rightarrow SO_4^{2-} + 4H^+ + 2e^-$		
	species	(1)	
	balance	(1)	3
4 (c) (i)	$VO_3^- + 6H^+ + 3e^- \rightarrow V^{2+} + 3H_2O$	(1)	1
4 (c) (ii)	$2VO_3^- + 12H^+ + 3Zn \rightarrow 2V^{2+} + 6H_2O + 3Zn^{2+}$		
	species	(1)	
	balance	(1)	2
			Total 9
5 (a) (i)	bromide: colourless to yellow/brown	(1)	
	iodide: colourless to dark brown and, with an excess of		
	chlorine, a black precipitate forms	(1)	2
5 (a) (ii)	bromide: cream precipitate	(1)	
	soluble in concentrated aqueous ammonia	(1)	
	iodide: a yellow precipitate	(1)	
	insoluble in concentrated aqueous ammonia	(1)	4
5 (b)	NaCl: steamy fumes	(1)	
	NaBr: steamy fumes	(1)	
	and brown fumes	(1)	
	$H^+ + Cl^- \rightarrow HCl$ or $H^+ + Br^- \rightarrow HBr$	(1)	
	$2Br^- + 4H^+ + SO_4^{2-} \rightarrow Br_2 + SO_2 + 2H_2O$		
	species	(1)	
	balance	(1)	6
			Total 12
6 (a)	falls from Mg to Ba	(1)	
	electron shells increases from Mg to Ba	(1)	
	outer electrons more shielded and less attracted	(1)	3
6 (b)	a white precipitate forms	(1)	
	no change or no precipitate	(1)	
	$Mg^{2+}(aq) + 2OH^-(aq) \rightarrow Mg(OH)_2(s)$	(1)	3
6 (c)	addition of calcium hydroxide increases soil pH	(1)	
	enabling different crops to be grown	(1)	2
6 (d)	barium sulfate is used to get X-ray images of digestive and bowel systems	(1)	
	barium sulfate is insoluble in water or body fluids	(1)	2
			Total 10

Question	Answer		Marks
7 (a)	acid rain	(1)	
	sulfur dioxide	(1)	
	absorb SO_2 using, e.g. CaO or convert into sulfuric acid	(1)	3
7 (b)	heating with carbon or CO	(1)	
	e.g. $2Fe_2O_3 + 3C \rightarrow 4Fe + 3CO_2$	(1)	
	heating with Na or Mg	(1)	
	$TiCl_4 + 4Na \rightarrow Ti + 4NaCl$	(1)	
	heating in hydrogen	(1)	
	$WO_3 + 3H_2 \rightarrow W + 3H_2O$	(1)	6
			Total 9
8 (a)	radical substitution	(1)	
	initiation $\quad Cl_2 \rightarrow 2Cl\cdot$	(1)	
	propagation $\quad CH_2Cl_2 + Cl\cdot \rightarrow \cdot CHCl_2 + HCl$	(1)	
	$\cdot CHCl_2 + Cl_2 \rightarrow CHCl_3 + Cl\cdot$	(1)	4
8 (b) (i)	$C_2H_6 + 2F_2 \rightarrow CH_3CHF_2 + 2HF$	(1)	1
8 (b) (ii)	uv radiation causes $CF_2Cl_2 \rightarrow \cdot CF_2Cl + \cdot Cl$	(1)	
	and the chlorine radicals then attack the ozone		
	$\quad Cl\cdot + O_3 \rightarrow ClO\cdot + O_2$	(1)	
	$\quad ClO\cdot + O_3 \rightarrow Cl\cdot + 2O_2$	(1)	3
8 (b) (iii)	C—F bonds are stronger than C—Cl	(1)	
	are less likely to be broken by uv	(1)	2
			Total 10
9 (a)	$CH_3CH_2Br + CN^- \rightarrow CH_3CH_2CN + Br^-$	(1)	
	propanenitrile	(1)	2
9 (b)	nucleophilic substitution	(1)	
	$NC\overset{-}{:}$	(1)	
	$CH_3\overset{\delta+}{CH_2} - Br^{\delta-} \longrightarrow CH_3CH_2CN + :Br^-$	(1)	3
9 (c)	reaction with chloroethane will be slower	(1)	
	C—Cl bonds are stronger than C—Br	(1)	2
			Total 7
10 (a)	E- isomer (1) Z-isomer (1)		
	there is restricted rotation about the double bond	(1)	
	there are two different groups on both ends of the double bond	(1)	4

Question	Answer		Marks
10 (b)	electrophilic addition	(1)	
	major product formed via secondary carbocation	(1)	
	which is more stable than alternative primary carbocation	(1)	7
			Total 11
11 (a)	$\Delta H = -235 - (-242 + 52.3)$	(1)	
	$= -45.3\ kJ\ mol^{-1}$	(1)	2
11 (b)	maximum yield formed at low temperature	(1)	
	and high pressure	(1)	
	but low temperature reaction is too slow to reach equilibrium	(1)	
	and high pressure equipment is expensive to build and to maintain	(1)	4
			Total 6
12 (a)		(1)	
		(1)	
	addition polymerisation	(1)	3
12 (b)	weak van der Waals forces between polymer chains	(1)	
	little energy required to overcome them	(1)	2
12 (c)	polyalkenes are not biodegradable	(1)	
	poly(propene) can be remelted and remoulded into new objects	(1)	2
			Total 7

Question	Answer	Marks
13 (a)	$C_6H_{12}O_6 \rightarrow 2C_2H_5OH + 2CO_2$ (1) yeast (1) aqueous solution (1) 35 °C (1)	4
13 (b)	(see table below)	4

Method	Rate of reaction	Quality of product	Raw material	Type of process
hydration	fast	pure	ethene from oil (finite resource)	continuous (cheap on manpower) (expensive equipment)
fermentation	slow	impure	sugars (renewable resource)	batch (expensive on manpower) (cheap equipment) (1)
	(1)	(1)	(1)	

		Total 8
14 (a)	$C_2H_5OH + 3CO_2 \rightarrow 2CO_2 + 3H_2O$ (1)	1
14 (b)	fermentation of one mole of glucose forms two moles of CO_2 together with two moles of ethanol (1) combustion of these two moles of ethanol produces another four moles of CO_2 (1) photosynthesis uses six moles of CO_2 to produce one mole of glucose (1) so there is no net production of CO_2 (1) but there will be energy considerations in the production of ethanol and its use (1) so there will be some overall carbon dioxide production (1)	6
		Total 7
15 (a)	$CH_3CH_2CH_2CH_2OH$ (1) butan-1-ol (1) primary (1) $\overset{OH}{\underset{}{|}}$ $CH_3CH_2CHCH_3$ (1) butan-2-ol (1) secondary (1) $H_3C-\overset{OH}{\underset{CH_3}{\overset{|}{\underset{|}{C}}}}-CH_3$ (1) methylpropan-2-ol (1) tertiary (1) $H_3C-\overset{H}{\underset{CH_3}{\overset{|}{\underset{|}{C}}}}-CH_2OH$ (1) methylpropan-1-ol (1) primary (1)	12
15 (b)	acid dichromate will turn from orange to green except with methylpropan-2-ol (1) the product of oxidation of butan-2-ol will not give a silver mirror, whereas the products of oxidation of butan-1-ol and methylpropan-1-ol will (1)	2
		Total 14

Question	Answer		Marks
16 (a) (i)	$C_4H_6O_3 = 102.0315$	(1)	1
16 (a) (ii)	$C_5H_{10}O_2 = 102.0678 = $ **X**	(1)	1
16 (a) (iii)	$C_3H_6N_2O_2 = 102.0428$	(1)	1
16 (b) (i)	carboxylic acid	(1)	1
16 (b) (ii)	$CH_3CH_2CH_2CH_2COOH$ (1) CH_3CHCH_2COOH (1) $\mid$ CH_3 $CH_3CH_2CHCOOH$ (1) CH_3 $\mid$ CH_3 $H_3C - C - COOH$ (1) $\mid$ CH_3		4
16 (b) (iii)	compare the fingerprint region of the infra-red spectrum of **X** with those of the four acids (1) an exact match will indicate which one is **X** (1)		2
			Total 10

The table below highlights aspects of *How Science Works* in the exemplar questions.

Question	How Science Works
1 (c) (ii)	data from different sources
2 (b)/(c)/(d)	causal relationships
3	industrial production – causal relationships
5	experimental activities
6 (d)	conflicting evidence
7	conflict between benefits of use of metals and environmental problems encountered during extraction
8	benefits of use of CFCs in refrigerators and harm to ozone layer/replacement by HFCs
11 (b)	compromise conditions
12	recycling of polymers
14	carbon neutral
16	use of experimental/spectroscopic data

Glossary

activation energy	the minimum energy required for a reaction to occur
allotropes	different structural modifications of an element
atomic number (Z)	the number of protons in the nucleus of an atom
atomic radius	half the distance between the nuclei of identical neighbouring atoms
backward (or reverse) reaction	one that goes from right to left in an equation
biofuel	fuel produced from renewable plant material (biomass)
bond dissociation enthalpy	the enthalpy change for the breaking of a covalent bond, with all species in the gaseous state
calorimeter	apparatus used to measure heat change
carbocation	a species which contains a carbon atom that has a positive charge
carbon neutral	applies to a process which occurs without any change in the total amount of carbon dioxide present in the atmosphere
catalyst	a substance which alters the rate of a reaction without itself being consumed
chain reaction	one in which many molecules undergo chemical reaction after one molecule becomes activated
chemical equilibrium	the point at which, in a reversible reaction, both the forward and backward reactions occur at the same rate, with the concentrations of all reactants and products remaining constant
Contact process	the industrial process used to manufacture sulfuric acid
disproportionation	a reaction in which the same species is simultaneously oxidised and reduced
dynamic reaction	one which proceeds simultaneously in both directions
elastic collisions	those in which no energy is lost on collision
electron shells	energy levels into which electrons are distributed
electronegativity	the power of an atom to attract the electrons in a covalent bond
electrophilic addition reaction	one in which a $C{=}C$ double bond becomes saturated; the mechanism involves initial attack by an electron-deficient species (electrophile)
elimination reaction	one in which an unsaturated compound is formed by the removal of a small molecule such as hydrogen bromide
endothermic	the gain of heat energy by a system; the enthalpy change is positive
endothermic reaction	one in which heat energy is taken in
enthalpy change (ΔH)	the amount of heat energy released or absorbed when a chemical or physical change occurs at constant pressure
exothermic	the loss of heat energy by a system; the enthalpy change is negative
exothermic reaction	one in which heat energy is given out

Fehling's solution	contains a deep blue copper(II) complex ion which, with aldehydes (but not ketones), is reduced, on warming, to form a red precipitate of copper(I) oxide
fingerprint region	the region below 1500 cm^{-1} in an infra-red spectrum
first law of thermodynamics	energy can neither be created nor destroyed, but can only be converted from one form into another
forward reaction	one that goes from left to right in an equation
free-radical substitution reaction	one in which the hydrogen atom of a C—H bond is replaced by a halogen atom; the chain-reaction mechanism involves attack on a neutral molecule by a radical (halogen atom)
greenhouse gases	gases in the atmosphere which absorb infra-red radiation (e.g. water vapour, carbon dioxide, methane and ozone)
Hess's law	the enthalpy change of a reaction depends only on the initial and final states of the reaction and is independent of the route by which the reaction occurs
homolytic fission	formation of radicals when a covalent bond breaks with an equal splitting of the bonding pair of electrons
integral mass	relative molecular mass to the nearest whole number
Le Chatelier's principle	a system at equilibrium will respond to oppose any change imposed upon it
mean bond enthalpy	the average of several values of the bond dissociation enthalpy for a given type of bond, taken from a range of different compounds
mechanism	the steps by which a reaction occurs
molecular fingerprint	the unique entire infra-red spectrum of an organic compound
molecular ion (M$^{+\bullet}$)	the species formed in a mass spectrometer by the loss of one electron from a molecule
nucleophilic substitution reaction	one in which an electron-rich molecule or anion (with a lone pair of electrons) attacks an electron-deficient carbon atom, resulting in the replacement of an atom or group of atoms originally attached to this carbon
oxidation	the process of electron loss
oxidation state (number)	the charge a central atom in a complex ion would have if it existed as a solitary simple ion without bonds to other species
product	a substance formed in a reaction
rate of reaction	the change in concentration of a substance in unit time
reactant	a substance consumed in a reaction
redox	used for reactions that involve both reduction and oxidation
reduction	the process of electron gain
reflux	a process in which a reaction mixture is heated in a flask fitted with a condenser to prevent the loss of volatile substances, including the solvent
reversible reaction	one which does not go to completion but can occur in either direction
standard conditions	usually taken as 100 kPa and 298 K

standard enthalpy of combustion	the enthalpy change, under standard conditions, when 1 mol of a substance is burned completely in oxygen, with all reactants and products in their standard states
standard enthalpy of formation	the enthalpy change, under standard conditions, when 1 mol of a compound is formed from its elements, with all reactants and products in their standard states
standard state	the normal, stable state of an element or compound under standard conditions, usually 298 K and 100 kPa
stereoisomers	are compounds which have the same structural formula but have bonds that are arranged differently in space
Tollens' reagent	contains the complex ion $[Ag(NH_3)_2]^+$ which, with aldehydes (but not ketones), is reduced, on warming, to silver
unsaturated	is applied to molecules which contain at least one $C{=}C$ double covalent bond or one $C{\equiv}C$ triple covalent bond
wavenumber	reciprocal wavelength $(1/\lambda)$ with units cm^{-1}, used to indicate band positions in infra-red spectra

Index

Notes

Notes

they had chosen seven soldiers. When they stepped forward confidently to face the old man, guns oiled and boots shiny, he looked down and shook his head. 'There is no one to attack us where I am going. Choose again, but be quick, for this is your last chance!'

In desperation, the people of Earth asked their greatest thinkers, poets, artists, politicians, mathematicians, musicians and sports people to help them choose and, in the nick of time, seven gardeners were chosen. When the old man appeared for a final time, everyone held their breath. Would he accept their final choice?

The old man looked at the gardeners, smiled a little, and then shook his head slowly. These were not the ones. 'The gardens will take care

of themselves where I am going,' he said solemnly. 'You have failed to choose wisely and now your planet and race will soon be gone forever.'

He turned away and began to float back to the purple star. However, just before he left the ground, a little boy pushed through the stunned crowds and grabbed his jacket.

'Mister, hey, Mister,' he squeaked, 'I know, I know who should go!'

The old man stopped to listen. The boy told him and the old man smiled and nodded.

About this story

It's sad to think that the context of this story is all too real. Parts of our world are struggling and suffering as it strains under the demands we are making of it. However, there are some very dedicated, talented and persuasive individuals and organisations who are trying to ease the burdens.

I hope that this story will plant seeds of inspiration in the minds of children and get them thinking about the world they are to inherit from us. This can lead to some positive explorations of how they, their families, their school, their community and so on are helping to improve or threaten this fragile inheritance.

Using this story

The big question

What does the little boy say to the old man?

Get thinking

Information processing

What has happened to Earth in the story?

Reasoning

What do you think has happened to Earth to cause it to be on the verge of dying in the story?

Enquiry

How is Earth in the story similar to our own planet?

Creativity

Create a different planet, one in which some of the problems of Earth have been solved. How did you solve them? Will this create any new problems?

Evaluation

Which group of people might be the worst that you could choose to go with the old man? Why do you think that this would be so?

Metacognition

Do you think that the old man cares about Earth?

Transfer

Think of a time when you have been in a position when you had to choose between different people. What happened? How did you choose and what were the results of your choice?

Think some more

Give each child a photocopy of page 122. Ask them to think about the dangers facing Earth and to record these on one side of the image. Next, ask them for some possible ways of helping to reduce or eliminate the dangers. You could use these points to develop practical steps that your children, their families and your school could adopt.

The Seven Children

Once there lived an elderly couple who had seven lovely children – four girls and three boys. All these children were happy, kind and hard working. But, despite this, their parents were not happy because each of the children had been born with a round hole in their middle. It was embarrassing having children like this as everyone in the town pointed and stared. They were desperate for their children to be complete, and so one morning they sent each child out to find a way to fill the hole in their middle.

The eldest girl, Ann, ran quickly to the market and packed her hole with the tastiest pies. The eldest boy, Baz, rushed off to meet his friends and filled his hole with their games, toys and laughter.

Two of the children walked to the seashore. Cass, the girl, placed shells, pebbles and seaweed in her hole and Dan, the boy, collected crabs and shrimps for his.

Another two children weren't sure what to do, so they sat down to think. After a while, the girl, Em, had so many thoughts that she decided to keep them in her hole. The boy, Fritz, found a quiet place to pray and let the prayers settle inside his.

The youngest child, Gail, was confused. She didn't really understand what she should be doing. So she went to see her grandmother and sobbed as she related what her parents had said. Her grandmother listened with the patience that only grandmothers have. When Gail had finished, her grandmother sat in silence for a while before holding her arms out wide. Gail rushed forwards and they hugged each other in the way only children and grandparents can. After they had squeezed themselves against each other middle to middle, the little girl ran home smiling.

When she got there, all her brothers and sisters were waiting. They wanted to see how everyone had filled their hole. Their parents carefully inspected what each child had done. They were pleased to see tasty pies; games and laughter; shells, pebbles and seaweed; crabs and shrimps; thoughts and prayers all sitting neatly in the different children's holes.

But they still missed the deep happiness they so wanted, as, although the holes were filled, people would still point and stare at what was inside.

Everyone turned to look at the youngest child. When they did so, they stopped and frowned because they couldn't see anything in her middle. If the older children's fillings and edges could be seen, then surely so should hers? Yet, Gail just was the little girl – no filling, no edges. Everyone demanded that she tell them how this was possible, but, of course, she had no idea.

About this story

This story explores what we need to make us emotionally resilient people. The love, warmth, acceptance and understanding that the youngest child received from her grandmother helped to give her the things she was lacking.

Using this story

The big question

How do you think the youngest girl's hole was filled?

Get thinking

Information processing

How did the other children fill their holes?

Reasoning

Why do you think the children's parents wanted their children to be complete?

Enquiry

The children were good and hard working, but their parents were not satisfied with them. Why do you think the children behaved so well despite this?

Creativity

What if the parents also had holes – how might they have filled them?

Evaluation

What do you think are the best and worst ways to fill holes like the ones in the story?

Metacognition

What might the people in the children's town have thought about them?

Transfer

When something goes missing, what can you do to try to find it?

If you don't know something, how can you find the answer?

This can give rise to some helpful learning strategies that can be displayed round the classroom as useful prompts.

What personal qualities would you like to develop?

Think some more

You could use a concept map to consider what some or all of the characters in the story might think about each other. Write the name of each character you want to consider in a separate circle. Add thought bubbles with text to indicate what a character is thinking about someone else. You can use arrows to indicate who is thinking what about whom. An example of a concept map for this story follows.

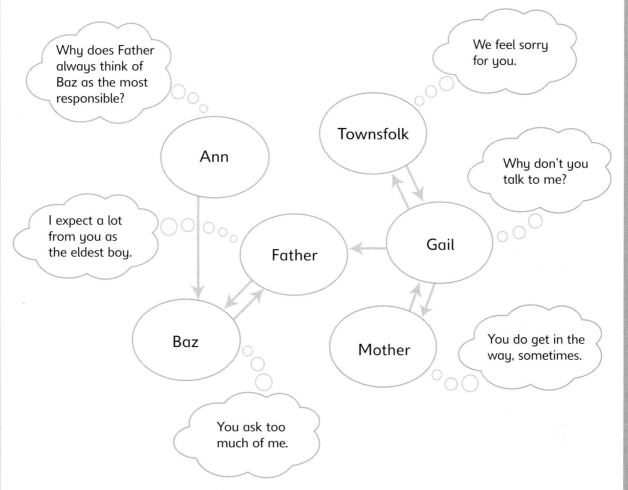

This thinking tool is useful to map out the possible thoughts of characters from:

- other stories;
- historical events;
- parties in a debate.

The Next Emperor

There was once a very old emperor who knew that he didn't have much longer to live, so he wanted to decide who was going to rule the empire when he was gone.

He called to his bedside his nine children, all of whom he loved, but none of whom he favoured. This meant that a difficult choice lay before him. To help him decide, the emperor set his children a task.

He said, 'You have one week to discover what the most important quality of a successful ruler is. Whoever finds it will rule my empire.'

Exactly seven days later, all nine children returned to their father's bedside to share what they had discovered.

The first boy stepped forward. He presented his father with a tiny flute. 'An emperor must be able to compose tunes and play them to his people. Music gives you the power to change how people feel. I claim the empire!'

Then the next child, a girl, gave the Emperor a book called *How to Rule Wisely and be Loved by Everyone*. 'A ruler needs to be able to talk to people well, listen to their views and persuade them to do things. They also need to write letters and read reports. I claim the empire!'

His third child now came before him holding a tiny flower. 'Father, an emperor must be able to understand nature; then he can care for his land and everything in it. I claim the empire!'

The Emperor's fourth child approached, bringing all her friends with her. 'A ruler needs to understand the people, knowing how to make them happy and how to look after them when they are sad. I claim the empire!'

The Emperor thought that all his children had chosen an important quality so far – he just couldn't decide which one was the best. Still, he had more of his children to hear, so he beckoned them forward.

The next child came alone and had no gift for his father. 'The most important quality an emperor needs is to understand himself. He must know what he is good at and what his weaknesses are, then he'll know how to rule wisely and when to ask for help. I claim the empire!'

The sixth child approached, holding a telescope. 'As well as looking carefully at everything nearby, a ruler needs to be able to look to the edges of their land. Then they must be able to see in their mind's eye what their empire will be like as it grows richer. I claim the empire!'

Next, the seventh child brought a counting machine. 'An emperor must understand numbers and how they work. He needs to be able to think, to plan what he's going to do next, and decide what's best for everyone. I claim the empire!'

Two more to go, thought the Emperor, and still no nearer a decision.

The eighth child threw him a statue of a dancer that she'd made. 'A ruler needs to keep fit and healthy, and to dance and to be skilled with their hands. Then they'll live a long life and the people who work with their hands will know they're understood. I claim the empire!'

Finally, the youngest, smallest and quietest child stepped forward. His comment was just as interesting as the others. 'An emperor must think deeply. He must know his place in the universe and never be afraid to ask big questions. I claim the empire!'

The Emperor looked at each of his children in turn, thinking very hard. He drew a deep breath and began to speak.

About this story

This is an abridged version of a story that I use when I'm working in schools. Acted out during an assembly, it introduces the idea of multiple intelligences (MI). This is a theory developed by Howard Gardner that states that there is a range of intelligences. Everyone has each of these intelligences to some degree. People tend to be stronger in some than others but, with the right training, the weaker intelligences can be developed.

After this story has been performed, the children take some lesson time, before an extra assembly at the end of the day, to decide who should be the next ruler. This helps them to reflect on the diversity of human skills and talents and to evaluate them one against another. For example:

- Is it more important to be able to use words effectively or to understand numbers?

- Are musical skills more useful than sporting prowess?

MI theory holds that we are all clever, but in different ways. It proposes that there are at least eight ways to be clever, each of equal value. Sadly, this is not a view that is common in society or in most school assessment systems.

This story provides a means to open up a discussion in this area and provides a route to valuing every skill in your classroom. The Emperor would be wise to realise that a little bit of all of his nine children would make a wonderful successor.

Using this story

The big question
What does the Emperor decide to do?

Get thinking

Information processing
What quality does each child say is the most important?

Reasoning
Pick three of the children and decide why each of them chose their particular quality.

Enquiry
How many different skills do you think there are in your class?

You could make a list to display in your classroom as a way to show the range of skills in your group.

Creativity
If the Emperor had three more children, what different qualities might they have suggested?

Evaluation
Can you make a list of the nine qualities, sorting them into an order of importance for being a good citizen?

Metacognition
What might the Emperor have been thinking about during the week that his children were away?

Transfer
What are your top three qualities or skills and which one do you think is the most important? Why do you think this?

Think some more

How could you use the different intelligences to retell this or any other story in this book? Here are two ideas for each of the intelligences.

Intelligence	Examples of how to use the intelligence
Musical/Rhythmic	• As a song • With sound effects
Verbal/Linguistic	• As a poem • As a radio report
Existential	• Condensing it into one difficult question • By asking why the characters behaved as they did
Naturalist	• By setting the story in a different place • By categorising the characters – good/evil, male/female, magic/human
Interpersonal	• By listing each character's strengths and weaknesses • As a play
Intrapersonal	• By writing a character's diary entry • By putting yourself in the story
Visual/Spatial	• By illustrating the story • By making a model of a character
Logical/Mathematical	• By working out the average word count per sentence • As a flowchart
Bodily/Kinaesthetic	• As a series of tableaux • By using plastic figures or similar toys to retell the story

The Magic Mirror

There was once a thief who stole a magic mirror. The wizard he stole it from was very angry, but he didn't chase the thief because he knew the mirror's dangerous power.

You see, anyone who caught a glimpse of themselves in the mirror would instantly split in two. Not a messy chop-down-the-middle split in two – oh no, the mirror was more subtle than that. The moment your eyes met those of your reflection, another you would suddenly appear right by your side.

However, you wouldn't recognise the other you. The other you would be horrible, twisted and unpleasant. The other you would be dirty and smelly. The other you would be made up of all the things you'd forgotten to do, or shouldn't have done, or should really have done, or had pretended to do when really you hadn't. This was the nasty you. And more often than not, this nasty you got angry with the real you and did something unrepeatable.

It wasn't wise to look in the magic mirror. Now you can understand why the wizard let the thief take it.

By now, the thief has carried the mirror all the way to his favourite place by the seashore. He sets it up in the sand, pulls off his shoes and socks, and stands to one side to admire the mirror's beauty.

Then he decides to stand in front of the mirror to look at his reflection. However, just as he moves into position, a big, noisy wave rushes up the beach and drenches his clothes. The thief is furious, although he doesn't know how lucky he is – the wave has saved him from being split in two.

The thief now wants to see how wet he looks and so he moves back towards the mirror to check. Suddenly a low-flying seagull appears and drops some revolting mess on his head. Yeuuck! It goes all over his hat and, because thieves never carry hankies, he can't clean himself up very well.

However, if he could see his reflection, he'd at least know the extent of the damage. So, for a third time the thief approaches the mirror, walking barefoot across the sand. As he does so, he stands on a sharp shell that cuts his foot, which hurts so much that the thief bends over in pain, swears loudly, grabs his sore foot and starts to hop.

As he's hopping around, bent over, swearing loudly, wet through, with a face of fury and a smelly hat, he topples in front of the mirror and looks up.

About this story

There's an episode in the original Star Trek series in which Captain Kirk gets split in two in a similar way to the thief. The bad Captain Kirk roamed the *Starship Enterprise* being utterly ruthless, while the good Captain Kirk spent his time being pleasant to everyone. Neither of the Kirks was fit to be the captain on their own, but when recombined as one at the end of the episode, the captain was fit – the message being that you need a bit of sensitivity and a bit of ruthlessness to be an effective starship captain.

You can use 'The Magic Mirror' with your children to think about opposites – the extremes that exist in human nature – and what problems might be caused if someone behaves only in ways at either end of the spectrum of good/evil, happy/sad, thoughtful/careless and so on.

Using this story

The big question
What happened when the thief finally looked in the mirror?

Get thinking

Information processing
What things stop the thief from looking in the mirror?

Reasoning
Why do you think the thief stole the mirror?

Enquiry
What other things do you think get included in the you that appears after looking in the magic mirror?

Creativity
Invent a magic mirror that does something strange when you look into it. What does it look like? What does it do? What are the consequences of staring into it?

Evaluation
In what way could the mirror you've created be useful?

Metacognition
If you were split in two by a magic mirror, what would the two yous be like? How would they get along?

Transfer
What opposites can you think of inspired by what's near you right now?

Think some more

With your children, look at the opposites in the table that follows. What might happen if they met? I have provided some suggestions to get you started. There are no definite answers to these puzzles, but they should give rise to some interesting discussions.

Try some opposites of your own with your children, using the photocopiable table on page 123.

Opposite 1	Opposite 2	Result of meeting
day	night	There would be dusk/dawn all the time
a screaming baby	a silent baby	Two screaming/silent babies
a smile	a frown	Both expressions on the same face? One expression winning over another, but which one is stronger?
freezing	boiling	Nice and warm
evil	good	A big question. Two evils? Two goods?

The Most Dangerous Beast

The most dangerous beast in the world is part dragon and part machine. Pipes and wires poke out from its greasy, scaly hide; while, inside, wheels and axles turn and grind alongside organs and veins. Its heart pumps blood and oil through a brain that ticks with tiny cogs and throbs with grey jelly. This beast is the Metacog – it knows what you're thinking.

'But hang on,' I hear you say, 'what's so dangerous about that? It's got no sharp teeth or knife-like claws. No fiery breath or poisonous bite.' Oh no, this beast is much more terrifying than that. If you get within one mile of the Metacog, it'll read your mind. It'll download your desires, suck out your strengths, pull out your plans and lever up your longings right into its own head. That's how it stays alive, by stealing others' thoughts, then leaving them for dead. There's no escape once you're in range. You might as well sit down and accept your fate.

And there's no way to destroy the Metacog. It'll know your plan of attack, your strengths and your escape route as soon as you are under a mile away. It'll have seen them forming in your mind.

Or is there a way to kill it?

This is a question to which the other slightly less dangerous beasts wanted to know the answer. With the Metacog around, humans weren't scared of normal monsters: the dragon, the troll, the blood mumbler, the skin stretcher,

in the World

the rock demon, the knife gloom and the moon gripe. They were tired of playing second fiddle to the Metacog and they wanted it dead.

They decided one by one to take on the Metacog.

First the dragon breathed fire from just over a mile away. The flames were fierce but did not travel far enough. The Metacog took one step towards the dragon and looked into its mind. It sensed the dragon's fear about its soft belly and reacted, throwing a metal spike. It hit the dragon with lethal accuracy, killing it in an instant.

The troll tried next. It blundered straight into the Metacog's trap with its club raised high and its trousers falling down. The Metacog found very little in the troll's brain and so, as it came closer, the Metacog held up a mirror. The troll screamed in terror at its own reflection and ran away. It kept on running, right off the edge of a cliff.

The blood mumbler was clever. Its singing could tame your blood, making it flow the wrong way, boil and bubble, or stop and start in response to

its tuneful commands. It began its song from two miles away but the melody was carried away by the wind. It came closer and closer to the Metacog, singing all the time, hoping to stop its blood and oil before it was too late.

The blood mumbler didn't stand a chance. The Metacog leapt into its brain and shattered the song. It pushed the notes backwards, sending them deep into the blood mumbler's mind, stopping its blood and leaving it lifeless.

The skin stretcher and the rock demon decided to work as a team. The skin stretcher could stand in one place and stretch part of its body for miles. The rock demon could sink into a rock and then burst it apart from the inside like a bomb. They made a dangerous pair.

The rock demon settled inside a boulder. Keeping its head out of the Metacog's range, the skin stretcher picked the boulder up and stretched its arms towards the most dangerous beast. However, as the rock demon was carried nearer, the Metacog realised that it wasn't really the skin stretcher's friend. It was a partnership of convenience and the rock demon was planning to kill the skin stretcher once the Metacog was dead. So the Metacog stepped within range of the skin stretcher and put this thought in its head.

In the fight that followed, the skin stretcher and the rock demon forgot all about the Metacog, killing each other in their anger.

The Metacog chuckled. There were only two beasts left: the moon gripe and the knife gloom. What could they possibly do?

About this story

If anyone uses the word 'metacognition' in a conversation with you, there are a number of things you can do:

- Nod thoughtfully and pretend you understand.
- Say 'Oooo, listen to you!'
- Reply 'I know an interesting story about that word!' and watch the look of smugness leave their face.
- Run away.

'Metacognition' means thinking about thinking and is really only a concise way to describe the skills of reflecting on and evaluating your own thought processes. The story of the Metacog is a memorable way to introduce this notion to your children. It's a very valuable skill to offer them.

Using this story

The big question
What might the knife gloom and the moon gripe do?

Get thinking

Information processing
What is the Metacog?

Reasoning
Why are the other beasts not happy?

Enquiry
How might the beasts work together in a team to fight the Metacog?

Creativity
Invent three other beasts that could fight the Metacog. What are their names and skills? What do they look like?

Evaluation
Which of the beasts in the story do you think is the least dangerous and why?

Metacognition
Invent a simpler word that means the same as 'metacognition'.

Transfer
Is it possible to tell what other people are thinking from their faces? What clues can help with this?

This is a very helpful exercise in developing your children's emotional intelligence. The findings can be used regularly in activities in this area.

Think some more

ORANGE thinking is a helpful thinking tool. Below is a table to show how it might be used to work out possible ways to defeat or limit the power of the Metacog.

O	Omit something	Try to omit any thoughts – making your mind blank or filling it with a distraction, such as saying the alphabet backwards, before approaching the Metacog.
R	Reduce something	Reduce the need to kill the Metacog by going to live in another story where the Metacog can't go.
A	Ask something	Ask a brain scientist how to defeat the Metacog.
N	Nudge something	Persuade lots of other beasts to go near to the Metacog. While it's occupied with them, you attack.
G	Grow something	Grow a field of corn and use the harvest to make a loaf of bread. Ask a wizard to enchant the bread so that the Metacog's powers will be limited if it eats it. Offer the bread to the Metacog as a peace offering.
E	Embed something	Fire a thought scrambler into the Metacog's mind and attack while it is confused.

You can use ORANGE thinking to explore ways to adapt an existing piece of work, such as a story, a poem, a painting, a model, a design, a report, a dance, an essay, and so on.

Below is an example of how to do this with the fairy tale of the Three Little Pigs. This addresses the question of how the pig in the house of straw might have survived.

O	Omit something	Don't reply to the wolf's question about whether you are in or not.
R	Reduce something	Work with the other two pigs to build one house, using your straw for a thatched roof.
A	Ask something	Ask your friend the grizzly bear to stay.
N	Nudge something	Persuade the local animal park that they would be more successful if they had a wolf on show.
G	Grow something	Grow a thick hedge of thorns round your house to prevent the wolf getting near it.
E	Embed something	Let the wolf think you are large and fierce by using a different voice.

Snow Angels

Every flake of snow that falls to Earth is different. Like a fingerprint, each one is unique; and the reason one snowflake is never the same as another is that each one has been hand made by an angel – a snow angel.

During sunny and warm periods, snow angels spend their time designing new snowflakes. Then, when it turns cold and icy and snow is needed, they use their tiny, delicate hands to make their designs out of the smallest slivers of ice. They gently blow these snowflakes out of their hands and watch them float down to Earth.

Snow angels are peaceful. Snow angels are gentle. Snow angels are quiet. Snow angels are so nice that they can be a real pain.

Alfred wasn't like the other snow angels. He was bigger, taller and wider, with larger, heavier hands. He moved slowly and loved to talk. On top of all this, he hated making snowflakes. Those he did design were much simpler than the snowflakes of the other angels. When he blew them off his hands, they would plummet to Earth like hailstones rather than float like feathers.

Alfred was not suited to being a snow angel, but the chief snow angel insisted that he stick at it. The other snow angels looked at him with pity, but never encouraged him or offered to help. They left him to get on with his chunky designs and oversized shapes. Alfred just had to put up with it.

Now, you know that if you have to keep putting up with something that's not right for you – day after day, hour after hour, minute after minute – you will eventually do one of three things: suffer in silence, lose your patience and blow your top, or start to mess about. For example, if you are a boy who likes to think on the move and you keep getting told to sit still, or if you are a girl who enjoys talking and you always get told to be quiet, then, sooner or later, you'll get very cross, very sad, or very naughty.

What did Alfred do? Well, he started to mess around. He made unusual snowflakes: ones with rude words on them; ones made out of cornflakes, plastic, tin and spaghetti; and snowflakes shaped like bottoms. He lit fires under the clouds, melting the other angels' work.

He made himself sneeze so that he startled the angels, making them blow their snow to the wrong country. He made one huge snowflake that landed on France, completely covering the country. He even made snowflakes that flashed and said, 'Santa will be on holiday this Christmas.'

The chief snow angel was not impressed. He made Alfred sit on a tiny, delicate chair with a finger to his lips, and told him to write out the words 'I must not mess around. I must learn to make snowflakes like the other snow angels.' He was meant to write this a hundred times. However, as soon as the chief snow angel went away to praise the other snow angels, Alfred began his pranks once more.

Here are some of the snowflakes he made this time: he made one that told you how beautiful you are; he made another that hovered in the air and followed the first person it saw, but always kept just out of reach; he made snowflakes that would never melt; he made snowflakes that were very hot; he created others made of rubber; and even fashioned snowflakes that exploded like fireworks when they touched the ground.

The chief snow angel was not amused. However, he was the chief snow angel and was wise enough to realise that his first approach with Alfred had not worked. So he decided to try something different.

About this story

If you are aware of learning-style theory and practice, then you will recognise what is going on in this story. Alfred's preferred learning and working style is not recognised or appreciated by the chief snow angel. He has to work and learn in an environment that is contrary to his preferences. Alfred likes to talk, but the other snow angels work in silence. He is big and strong and enjoys moving around, but he has been given delicate tactile work to do. He feels uncomfortable and misunderstood, so he tries to exert a degree of control by being subversive and going underground.

Alfred's misbehaviour actually reveals his strength: he's a wonderfully creative individual. I wonder if the chief snow angel will recognise this and find a way to play to Alfred's strengths?

Using this story

The big question

What does the chief snow angel do with Alfred this time?

Get thinking

Information processing

What did Alfred do when he was messing around?

Reasoning

Why do you think the snow angels behaved as they did?

This question can be used to address the preferred learning style of the other snow angels, as well as their treatment of Alfred.

Enquiry

What do snowflakes look like close up?

A quick check through an Internet search engine should reveal a wealth of images of snowflakes.

Creativity

What other sorts of surprising snowflakes could Alfred make?

Evaluation

What do you think is the best thing that Alfred did when he was messing around? Why did you choose this?

Metacognition

How do you think Alfred got all his wonderful ideas?

This is a tricky question for children to understand at first, but it can reveal some interesting insights into what inspires your children.

Transfer

Have you ever felt like Alfred? What happened? How did you react?

Think some more

The ideas in 'Snow Angels' address important issues related to personalised learning –
how the individual learning preferences of children can be valued and used in the classroom.

The first step to achieving this is to find out what your children's learning preferences are.
On page 124 is a photocopiable activity that will help you to begin to match your teaching
styles with your children's learning styles. Ask each child to fill in a copy of this table, with
help if necessary. Once you have collated the responses, you may find some valuable details
that will have an impact on how you teach and how you expect your children to learn.

The House of Halves

When their mother and father died, Lianne and Rhianne divided the family house into two. Lianne took a thick blue pen and drew a line that started at the bottom of the front door, went up the outside wall, over the roof and all the way down to the back door. Rhianne used a tape measure to make sure that each half of the house was the same size. Lianne boarded up doorways and Rhianne built walls.

When the work was finished, Lianne went to live in the rooms on the left-hand side of the house and Rhianne had the ones on the right-hand side. Both of them were very sad and missed their parents bitterly.

From then onwards, everything was divided in half. When the postman brought letters and parcels, they were sliced down the middle; when the milk was delivered it was separated into two small bottles; and when the fishmonger brought trout, Lianne got the left side and Rhianne got the right, give or take a few bones.

Lianne occupied herself by organising her furniture and writing lists of things she needed to do. Rhianne spent her time daydreaming and thinking up wonderful new ideas.

As the weeks passed, Lianne got busier and busier, rearranging her tables and chairs twenty-four times a day at seven minutes past the hour. She also wrote a huge list to organise all the other lists that she'd already made. At the same time, Rhianne daydreamed and

hummed and had even bigger ideas – but she didn't bother about eating and drinking or tidying up.

After a year of this, Lianne was frantic. She couldn't sit still, she couldn't stop organising and she never slept. In the other side of the house, Rhianne was living in a waking dream, wandering aimlessly around her rooms, doing nothing but creating and imagining wonderful new things.

After ten years of living like this, Lianne was moving so quickly and doing so much that she was a blur. Rhianne had stopped wandering and just stood there imagining.

Then the walls of the house that had kept
them apart for so long began to fall down.
Very soon the house was no longer split
down the middle. Lianne could be seen rushing
round and Rhianne could be seen standing still.
Lianne whirled closer and closer to Rhianne
until, finally, she bumped right into her. It was
then that something curious happened.

About this story

It's a 'neuro-myth' that the two hemispheres of the human brain are in charge of different, separate sets of skills and dissimilar ways of thinking. However, left-brain and right-brain traits are distinct and give us a useful way of categorising behaviour.

Analytic (what was left-brain thinking) includes thinking logically, being objective, taking things literally and being organised. Holistic (what was right-brain thinking) covers thinking intuitively, being subjective and seeing the big picture. In both cases there are many associated features.

Favouring one type of thinking over another has even been linked to different genders. However, a more flexible description is now held to be accurate. This is that the brain is a plastic and dynamic network of numerous connections in which certain combinations of areas are associated with specific activities, although other areas can take over if they have to – for example in stroke victims who recover sight or speech.

The analytic-left traits and holistic-right traits are present in all of us, but in different combinations. Most of us can use a repertoire across the left–right spectrum, depending on what we're doing and with whom.

This story takes up the idea of a person living wholly by using aspects of one type of thinking. It could provoke some interesting work on evaluating the two types of thinking, seeing their benefits and drawbacks.

You might find it helpful to consider your own teaching style. Is it more analytic or holistic? What about how you structure the curriculum? Is it generally left or right? What implications are there if you are a right-brained teacher in a left-brained school or vice versa?

Using this story

The big question

What happened when Lianne and Rhianne collided?

Get thinking

Information processing

What did Lianne do in her half of the house?

Reasoning

Why do you think that Rhianne behaved in the way that she did?

Enquiry

What do you think Lianne's and Rhianne's parents were like?

Why do you think Lianne and Rhianne decided to live in separate parts of the house?

Creativity

If there had been a third child and the house had been split into three, how might this child have behaved?

Evaluation

Who do you think behaved in the most interesting way, Lianne or Rhianne, and why?

There is clearly no definite answer to this question, but the discussion it provokes can lead to some interesting evaluations of the different thinking types.

Metacognition

What might Rhianne think of Lianne and Lianne think of Rhianne?

Transfer

Who are you most like, Lianne or Rhianne?

Identifying a learning preference is beneficial as it helps a child to become aware of their strengths as well as areas they could develop.

Think some more

Give each child a photocopy of page 125 and ask them to tick which activity Lianne or Rhianne would be more likely to do. It may be that some of the activities will be done by both sisters. You could sort the activities into a Venn diagram of two overlapping circles: one circle for Lianne, one for Rhianne, and the overlapping section for both.

This exercise can lead to a lot of fruitful debate about how the activities are allocated.

Butterfly Man

There was once a cruel and greedy man who collected butterflies. He loved the excitement of chasing them with his huge butterfly net. When he caught them, he would kill them with a long, shiny pin and put them in little boxes with glass fronts.

He caught red ones and blue ones, green ones and yellow ones, ones with stripes and ones with spots, ones that shone in the sun and ones that hid in the trees. He travelled the world to find butterflies, visiting remote, humid forests and green, chalky meadows. Once he returned home, he would display the butterflies and charge visitors £15 to look at them – in their little boxes with glass fronts.

One day a young boy came to look at the butterflies. After wandering round for a while, he went up to the collector and said, 'Hey, I don't reckon much to your butterflies!' The man stared at the boy open mouthed. He thought his collection was the best in the land. But the boy didn't. 'They're all boring,' he said, 'not like the butterflies I know.'

The man demanded to know about these butterflies that the boy knew. The boy smiled helpfully and offered to show him. So the man grabbed his kit, got hold of the boy's ear, twisted it between his finger and thumb, and marched him out of the house. This was unnecessary as the boy was quite willing to share his butterflies. Twisting the boy's ear just made the man feel strong and important.

The boy led the man into a nearby garden, where he pointed at a bright green bush. There in the middle of the bush rested a wonderful butterfly. The man raised his net and his largest shiny pin, ready to strike, when the boy said, 'Stop! That's not it – watch!' They peered at the butterfly and saw it lay a tiny egg, before flying away.

'What on earth is that?' shouted the man, thinking he'd been tricked.

'Just wait,' said the boy.

After a while the egg split open slowly and a tiny caterpillar squeezed its way out. The man had never paid

much attention to caterpillars before and was curious about its striped body and funny walk. But not so curious that he'd forgotten about the butterfly he'd been promised.

'Where's my butterfly?' he hissed through clenched teeth.

'Just wait,' said the boy.

So they waited and waited. They watched the caterpillar eat leaves, stalks and then more leaves. They watched it grow fatter and fatter, shedding its skin as it went. Finally, they watched it hide itself in a leaf-shaped pod and attach itself to a branch.

'What on earth is going on?' asked the man, realising he was quite amazed by what he had seen.

'Just wait,' said the boy.

They waited in breathless excitement. The man had lowered his net by now, but his pin was still at the ready. Unnoticed by them, the sun sunk below the skyline and stars began to appear. Then, just as night was falling, the chrysalis shook. It wobbled and swung. It swayed and stretched. Slowly a crack grew along it and the most beautiful butterfly in the world struggled out.

The butterfly that laid the egg had been wonderful, but this one seemed a hundred times brighter and more magnificent. It was all the colours the man had seen and some he'd only read about. Its wings were made from the most complicated patterns that nature could conjure up. And it glowed like it was on fire. This butterfly would surely make the man's collection the best in the whole world. He drew back his pin quickly and was about to stab the butterfly when the boy said in a quiet voice, 'Just wait.'

About this story

The butterfly is a familiar metaphor for learning, change and growth. It has great value as it reminds us of how children wrestle with learning, both inside and outside the classroom.

You can use this story to help your children think not only about what they are learning, but about how they are learning it. It provides a chance to reflect on progress and to celebrate achievements.

The butterfly man is an unpleasant character. However, will he change into a better person?

Using this story

The big question
What does the butterfly man do next – does he strike or wait?

Get thinking

Information processing
What different sorts of butterfly does the man collect?

Reasoning
Why do you think that people collect and display butterflies?

Enquiry
How would you try to persuade the man to stop killing beautiful things?

Creativity
Choose any living thing and invent a way in which it could change into another living thing, like a caterpillar becoming a butterfly.

Evaluation
Do you think the boy should have acted differently? If so, how?

Metacognition
What thoughts might the man have had during his time by the bush?

Transfer
In what ways have you changed in the last year?

Think some more

I should like to thank Margaret Byrne for the following short, simple activity.

Two caterpillars looked up and saw a beautiful butterfly flying overhead. One turned to the other and said . . .

Ask your children to complete this sentence in at least five different ways. For example:

- 'Will we ever be like that?'
- 'You'll never get me up in one of those things!'
- 'What on earth is that?'
- 'Looks like number 62 is out of nectar again.'
- 'Do you fancy a bit of a flutter?'

Story without Words

About this story

As well as thinking in words, we can also think in pictures: words can trigger pictures in our minds. This is why some people baulk at screen adaptations of books they have read – they already have a strong visual image of the story and a film can shatter this personal representation.

There are nine illustrations for the story without words. The story itself has yet to be written. Each child in your group needs a copy of page 104. They need to study it and consider what story they see. More is involved here than a sequencing exercise. When your children begin to link up images into a story, it will be an original version. There are many, many equally right and creative answers.

You can choose to modify this story to match the needs of your children. See the 'Creativity' section that follows.

Using this story

The big question

What story did you make up and how did it compare with that of others in the group?

Get thinking

Information processing

Describe each illustration using up to three sentences. These can be written or spoken.

Reasoning

Choose a theme and draw lines between illustrations that include this theme. For example, you could connect pictures that have a pair of eyes looking at you or that have an old man in them.

Enquiry

If you looked to the left and right of each picture, what would you see? This can be done in terms of time and/or in terms of space – the narrative and the scene.

Creativity

Create a story using the illustrations. Here are some creativity rules to help. Choose one to structure the activity before you begin.

- Use all of the pictures in any order.
- Use a limited amount of pictures.
- Add up to three pictures of your own.
- Add something to three of the pictures.
- Make up a rule of your own.

Evaluation

Which of the creativity rules might be the most useful and why?

Compare two stories that have been made using the same rule. Which one did you enjoy the most and why?

Metacognition

Look at one of the illustrations from the story with a partner. Each of you writes or draws in secret what you think might happen next. Compare your answers. How were they different? Why do you think they were not exactly the same?

Transfer

Illustrate a week of your life with nine pictures. These can be shared out afterwards and other children can see what narratives they create using the pictures.

Think some more

Ask your children to get into pairs. Give each pair a copy of the story cut up into the separate illustrations. One child in each pair shuffles their illustrations and lays them on the table one at a time. After the first illustration is laid down, the children in the pair take it in turns to make a connection between the next illustration and the previous one. The connections can be simple, such as both illustrations have a tree; or more subtle, such as both have elements of magic in them. A narrative link which builds part of a story can also be made.

The Magic Helter Skelter

On a small patch of wasteland in the middle of a busy town, the magic helter skelter stands unnoticed. No one pays attention to its peeling paintwork and rotting wood as they hurry by, living their busy lives. No one hears it creak in the wind as they chatter endlessly about this, that and the other. No one knows that it doesn't cast a shadow, however much the sun tries to make one.

If only someone would stop for a while, climb its squeaking steps and take a ride down its spiralling slide. If only – but sadly it seems that everyone has too much to do.

However, if you're not in a rush, things might be a lot different.

And on this particular day, Kelly wasn't in a rush at all. In fact, she was deliberately going slowly. She was taking pies to her mad uncle who lived on the other side of town. She didn't enjoy this weekly errand, watching her uncle grab the pies without a word of thanks and slamming the door in her face. But Kelly's mother insisted.

So each week Kelly took her time, delaying the moment when she had to knock on her uncle's door. She went in all sorts of directions through the town, sometimes even going the wrong way on purpose. It was on such an occasion that she came across the small patch of dirty grass and discovered the magic helter skelter.

Kelly put her basket on the ground and looked at the slide. She thought it was a perfect reason to put off delivering the pies. She carefully stood on the first step, which seemed strong enough. So with growing confidence Kelly climbed to the top. She grabbed a mouldy, frayed mat from a pile, sat on it and launched herself down the slide.

As Kelly flew down the slide, she soon realised that this helter skelter was not like the ones she had ridden on before. On those ones you would shoot off the bottom in a few seconds. On this one, a minute had already passed and, although she was sliding faster and faster, she hadn't reached the ground. Another minute went by and she was still flying round and round, and down and down. With no end in sight, Kelly began to enjoy the ride less and less.

Kelly began to think, 'What if it never ends? What if I'm stuck here, going round and round, for ever?' By now, she was very scared. She was scared of the magic at work and cried out, 'Please make it stop. Please let me off – I'll go straight to my uncle's house and never dawdle again. I promise, just let me off!' But it didn't help – if anything, Kelly went faster still. This made her angry and she jammed her feet hard against the edges of the slide to try to slow herself down. 'Stop, you stupid thing!' she screamed.

At that, the helter skelter replied, 'Be quiet and keep your feet off me! People shouldn't try to slow down.' This was a shock for Kelly, but she soon gathered herself together enough to say, 'Why won't you let me off?' But the helter skelter remained silent. Kelly thought she might be released if she did what the slide asked. Tucking her feet back on the mat, she felt the air rush past her faster.

She called for help but no one heard; she pinched her arm in case she was dreaming; she even turned around on the mat, hoping she would go up the slide, but she still carried on down.

'This isn't fair,' Kelly thought. 'I haven't done anything wrong! I've tried as hard as I can and done everything I can think of, but you're not being fair! Why won't you let me off?'

Then, all of a sudden, she landed with a bump on the area of patchy grass at the bottom of the slide.

As she walked quickly away clutching her basket of pies, Kelly thought she heard the voice of the helter skelter say, 'Well done, Kelly. You passed the test.' But she couldn't be sure, and she hadn't a clue what the test was.

About this story

There are a number of themes involved in this story, as you will see from the questions that follow. One of these is a link between the helter skelter and spiral dynamics. Spiral dynamics is a concise method of exploring how individuals, schools, organisations, communities and even nations grow and evolve naturally over time. It provides clear frameworks for improving organisations, developing better communication, giving guidance on effective leadership and enhancing interpersonal relations.

If you want to know more, there is a wealth of information on the Internet about spiral dynamics. Type it into a search engine and see what you find.

Using this story

The big question

What test had Kelly passed?

Get thinking

Information processing

In what ways does Kelly react to the helter skelter?

Reasoning

Why don't you think anyone else sees the helter skelter?

Enquiry

What different fairground rides can you think of, both old and new?

Creativity

Take two different fairground rides and combine them into a new ride – for example: dodgems on a bouncy castle or the ghost train down a helter skelter. The children could draw or make models of these inventions.

Evaluation

Do you think the helter skelter is good or evil, and why?

Metacognition

Can you make a connection between the helter skelter and Kelly's uncle?

There is no definite answer here, but a number of possibilities.

Transfer

What do you do when you feel trapped or when you don't have control?

This discussion can provide a good list of strategies that the children can utilise in the future.

Think some more

Give each child a copy of the spiral on page 126. Ask them to answer the questions as they follow the spiral. Their answers, whether written or drawn, will provide you and them with some interesting insights.

The Wish Camel

One cold and starry winter's night, a wish camel appeared next to a church in a village. This was a fortunate event because wish camels are very rare and choose their paths with care, avoiding people where possible. When wish camels do appear, they stay no more than a day before vanishing.

In the morning the children of the village discovered the camel standing in the crisp sunlight, chewing lazily on some weeds it had pulled from the roadside. They rushed around it excitedly and stroked its wiry fur.

The adults were puzzled by the children's game. As you may know, adults can't see wish camels and so they found the children's story hard to believe.

I suppose you're wondering by now what's so special about wish camels. Perhaps you think you've got a pretty good idea already, but just to make sure, I'll tell you.

When you sit on a wish camel and face forwards, you are allowed one wish to change the *future*. When you sit on a wish camel and face backwards, you are allowed one wish to change the *past*. However, you only get one wish. If you make the wrong wish, you'll have to wait for the wish camel to return to try to sort it out, and that can take years.

The children of the village formed a line and got ready to climb up between the camel's humps to make their wishes.

James was first. He'd found a step ladder in the churchyard and rested it against the camel's warm flank. He climbed up and sat facing forwards. 'I wish I could fly!' he whispered into the camel's ear. A strange lightness came over his body as James climbed down from the camel's back. He ran off to the nearby woods to explore what this meant in private.

Ella quickly took James's place, but she sat looking backwards. 'I wish I'd practised harder at swimming,' she said. No sooner had she spoken than she felt herself growing taller, leaner and stronger, just as if she had practised harder at her swimming. She ran off to the village's small swimming pool to try out her new body.

Next up the ladder came the twins: Kathryn and Emily. They squeezed themselves between the wish camel's humps, facing forwards. Together they said, 'We want to be different and the same all at once.' There and then Kathryn turned into Emily and Emily turned into Kathryn, although very few people noticed the difference.

Now it was Matthew's turn. When he reached the top of the ladder, he sat facing neither backwards nor forwards, but sideways. 'I want something for someone else,' he said. 'I wish for my brother to have hair like mine – lots and lots of it, all over.' It was an interesting wish and, a few streets away, in a small house,

a baby suddenly felt his hair grow, curl over his shoulders and flow down his back.

Finally Beth climbed up and faced backwards. She thought for a while, and then said to the camel, 'I wish that I'd met you nine years ago' – she was 9 and a bit years old. And there she was, a tiny baby, cosy, asleep and dreaming between the wish camel's humps.

Once the wish camel had returned Beth to her bed through her open window, it went on its mysterious way.

Many years passed. The children grew up and became very nearly, but just not quite, adults.

And on another cold and starry winter's night, the wish camel returned.

James, Ella, Kathryn, Emily, Matthew and Beth were all roused from their sleep. Without quite knowing why, they each rushed out of their homes. Seeing the wish camel – remember they were still children in some ways – they rushed up to it. They knew that this was their chance to make another wish. One at a time, they grabbed the camel's neck and clambered between its humps. Each wish of these nearly-but-not-quite adults was for the same thing – the exact opposite of what they wished for all those years ago.

Now why do you think that was?

About this story

The question at the end of this story gives you and your children an opportunity to develop your creative reasoning skills by thinking about the implications of having wishes granted. You'll know from fairy tales that, even with three wishes, things can go horribly wrong. For example:

Husband (eagerly): I wish I had a big, juicy sausage to eat!

A big, juicy sausage appears.

Wife (angrily): You idiot! What a waste of a wish. I wish that sausage was stuck on your nose.

The sausage leaps onto the husband's face.

Husband (aghast): I wish it was gone! Now!

Sausage disappears.

There are the three wishes wasted, along with all the potential for health, wealth and happiness.

The wish camel allows children to change one thing in their future or one thing in their past. However, none of the children in the story appears to consider the consequences of their wish before they make it.

We can guess that events don't turn out as expected because each of the children wants to undo things when the wish camel returns. Maybe James could fly, but was unable to walk on the ground again. Perhaps Ella became a mermaid at dawn every day. Maybe Kathryn and Emily became four people, then eight and so on. Possibly Matthew's brother's hair would not stop growing. What if every time Beth had a birthday, she became a baby for the day?

Using this story

The big question

Why do you think each of the children wanted to reverse their wish?

Get thinking

Information processing

What do you think each of the children requested when the wish camel returned?

Reasoning

Why do you think the children chose the things they did when they first made a wish?

Enquiry

What questions might the children have asked the camel before they made their wishes?

Creativity

Wish camels don't necessarily have to be the only animals that grant wishes. Think up another. How many wishes does it give? To whom? Is there anything special or dangerous about it?

Evaluation

Which child do you think made the most useful wish?

Metacognition

What do you think the adults in the story think of what the children say about the wish camel?

Transfer

What would you wish for if you had the chance to sit on a wish camel and you knew that it was coming back at the same time next year?

Think some more

Carry out a wish survey of fairy tales and other well-known stories. In each one, find out the following:

- Who grants the wishes?
- How many wishes were granted?
- Who got the wishes?
- Is the outcome good or bad?

'Cinderella', 'The Fisherman and his Wife' and 'Aladdin' are good ones to start with.

Photocopiable resources

The ripple effect

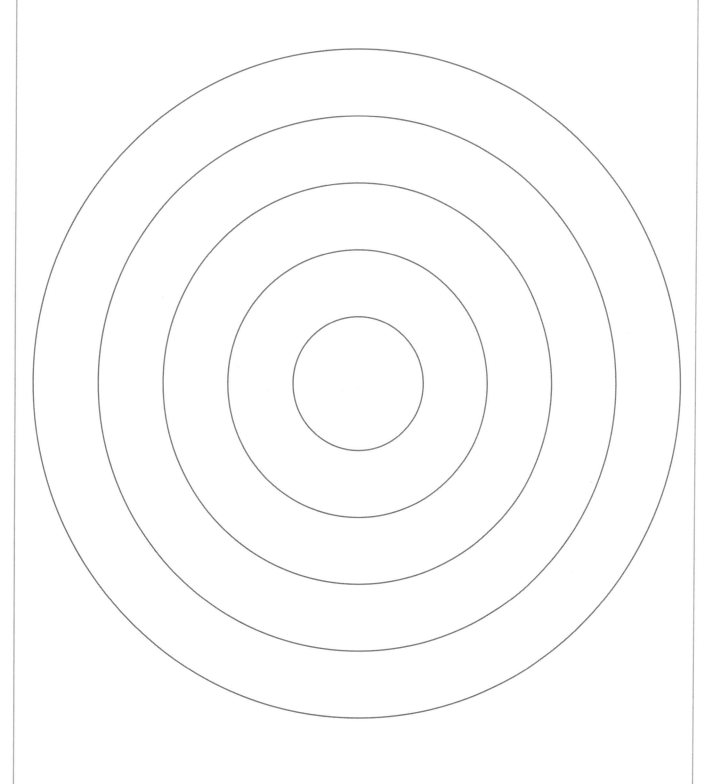

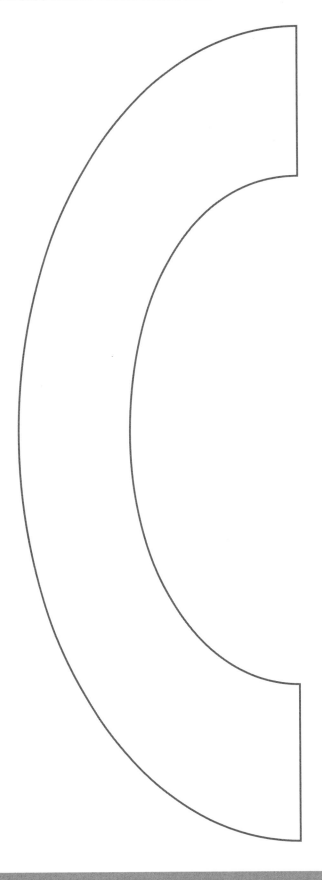

Your story

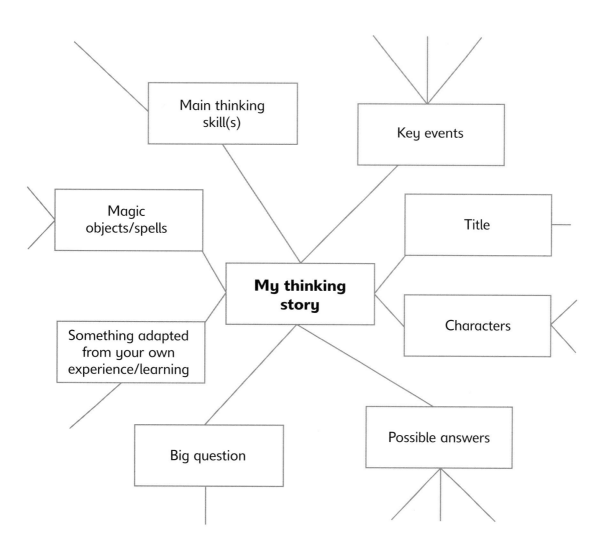

Main thinking skill(s)

Key events

Magic objects/spells

Title

My thinking story

Characters

Something adapted from your own experience/learning

Possible answers

Big question

Permission to Photocopy

Venn diagram

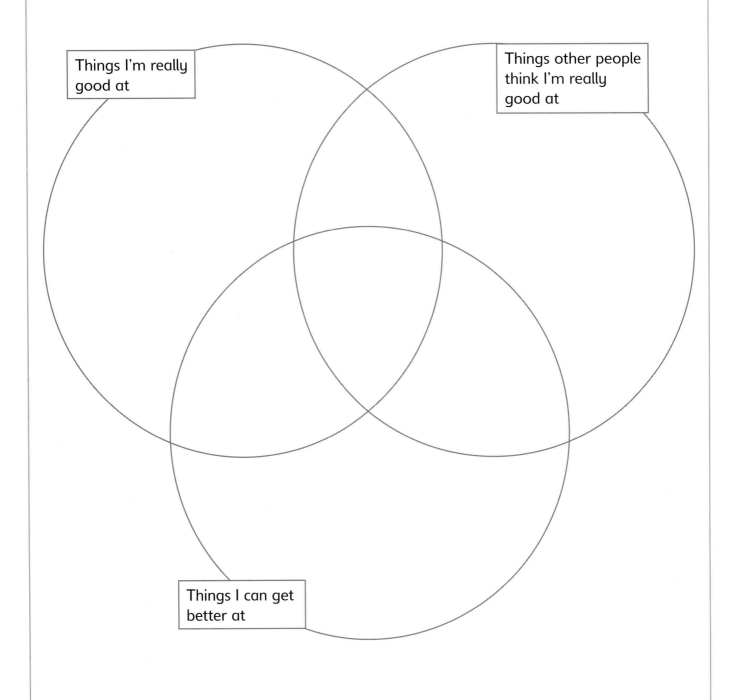

Things I'm really good at

Things other people think I'm really good at

Things I can get better at

PMI thinking

Plus	Minus	Interesting

CCC thinking

Consequences	Consequences

Choice	Choice

Challenge

Choice	Choice

Consequences	Consequences

Pros and cons

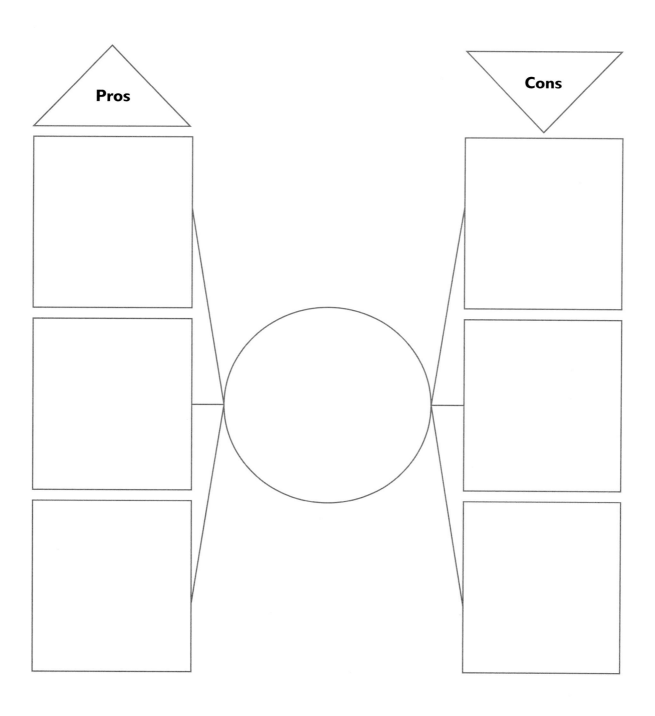

Caring for the planet

Dangers

....

....

....

....

....

....

....

....

....

....

....

....

....

....

....

Help

....

....

....

....

....

....

....

....

....

....

....

....

....

....

When opposites meet

Opposite 1	Opposite 2	Result of meeting

Preferred learning style

Ring the number that best describes how you feel about each statement. 1 is strongly agree and 5 is strongly disagree.

When I'm working I like to . . .					
. . . be warm.	1	2	3	4	5
. . . be able to talk to my friends.	1	2	3	4	5
. . . work on my own.	1	2	3	4	5
. . . have something interesting to look at.	1	2	3	4	5
. . . have something interesting to listen to.	1	2	3	4	5
. . . have something interesting to touch.	1	2	3	4	5
. . . have the lights dim.	1	2	3	4	5
. . . sit somewhere comfortable.	1	2	3	4	5
. . . get up and move about.	1	2	3	4	5

The House of Halves

Tick whether you think Rhianne, Lianne or both would be likely to do each activity.

Activity	Lianne	Rhianne
Make the bed.		
Do the washing up.		
Paint a picture.		
Help a friend.		
Arrive on time.		
Go exploring.		
Try a new kind of food.		
Write a poem.		
Fall in love.		
Arrive late.		
Climb a tree.		
Cry.		
Sing and dance.		
Go to the library.		
Get into trouble at school.		
Have a pet.		
Eat the same food every day.		
Flick between television programmes.		
Play the guitar.		
Pray.		
Have lots of friends.		
Use a calculator.		
Go swimming.		

Spiral thinking

What do you do to help other people?

What would you most like to do?

What rules do you follow?

What makes you angry?

What would you pray for?

What are you scared of?